ENDORSE.

"Margaret Donna Pleasant Soaries is an unusual woman of faith who from her teenage years elected to spend her time in national evangelism efforts, private and corporate worship, and even an occasional all-night prayer service. She speaks humbly, wisely and with a gift to engage her listeners as if they were seated at her kitchen table. She is that quintessential Proverbs 31 woman and that 21st century prayer warrior that we all aspire to be!"

Rev. Dr. Melinda Contreras-Byrd
Psychologist, Adjunct Professor at New Brunswick Theological Seminary

"Donna Soaries has always been a fierce advocate for the power of prayer, and a mother's prayer in particular. Her innovative "Mothers Determined To Pray" prayer calls made real her belief in the collective power of mothers lifting their words to God. Her book is another empowering moment of realization, and an invigorating and revelatory reminder that prayer is an irreplaceable resource for women blessed with the triumphs and trials of motherhood. Nothing makes you pray more than being a mother, and Donna Soaries offers a roadmap."

Congresswoman Bonnie Watson Coleman
Member of U.S. House of Representatives

"This book is a delightful love offering. There is something especially effective about the passionate prayers of a persistent mother who trusts God's plans for her children. The earnestness reflections in these pages, are the sacred sentiments of a woman who is deeply acquainted with the joys, rewards and sorrows of parenting in every season of life. The thoughts here are mined from a deep well of experience, which are satisfyingly saturated with love, wisdom and grace that can only flow from a mother's heart. You will be captivated and inspired by the teachings of this woman of excellence, who loves God and family with all her heart, mind and strength."

Rev. Sheleta E. Fomby
Co-Leader of New Life Campus, Reid Temple AME Church

"This wonderful book is a special blessing for all mothers who have spent time worrying about and praying for our children. Donna Soaries inspires us with prayer, scripture, humor, love, and touching stories from her own life experience. She takes us on a journey through the joyful moments and encourages us as we raise children in these challenging times. As a beacon of hope, this book will be a healing lifeline for all mothers as we "pray without ceasing" for all of the children in our lives."

Nancy Boyd-Franklin, Ph.D.
Distinguished Professor of Psychology, Rutgers University

"As a mother, grandmother and great grandmother who has known the struggle of inner city living, I am comforted by your faith in God's Word. Isaiah 66:13 (NIV) "As a mother comforts her child so will I comfort you." I have been on the Mothers Determined To Pray prayer call since it began. In the early years, I would call in from Thousand Oaks, California at 5am! Indeed, Donna, you have discovered the "wind beneath your wings" that intervening variable, the Holy Spirit. Pray on! Fly on! Donna, you are soaring!"

Rev. Doris Sherman, Retired Presbyterian Pastor

"It was such a pleasure being raised by a strong, intelligent woman who always lived up to her maiden name, Pleasant. She genuinely enjoys being a mother despite the challenges and uncertainties that she could not have prepared for. This book is a reminder of how far love and prayer can take you in life, not just as a mom but also as a human being. Any member of any family can relate to this book in their own way!"

Malcolm Soaries

"O Lord! I'm so glad my mom decided to share her gift of storytelling. She absolutely loves being a mom, even gave up a whole singing career to become one! That's why you'll enjoy this because it's so genuine."

Martin Soaries

"The keys to motherhood as exemplified by Donna Soaries begin with kindness, compassion and acceptance. Out of that comes divinely inspired guidance and nurturing with loving boundaries. These qualities are implicit in her writings and her life. The fact that Donna has taken the time to write this book, to teach and inspire us, is the ultimate in true mothering.-- Read and then reread this book."

Honey Sterzer RN, LCSW, BCN

"Donna Soaries is like an angel to me. She has appeared when I have needed someone to lean on. She and Pastor Soaries have been our rock. And through the years she has been a literal Mom to my players. All of this while she has managed to raise two fine young men who I love. I am sure her book will be as helpful to readers as she has been to me, my family and my teams."

C. Vivian Stringer
Hall of Fame Head Coach, Rutgers University Women's Basketball Team

O Lord!

Reflections
of a
Praying Mother

O Lord!

Reflections
of a
Praying Mother

DONNA SOARIES

Faith in Action Publishing

O Lord! Reflections of a Praying Mother

Published by Faith in Action Publishing
Printed in the United States of America
First Printing

ISBN-13: 978-0-9972436-3-5
ISBN-10: 0-9972436-3-5

This book is dedicated to the
loving memory of my parents
Edith Henrietta Humbert Pleasant
and William Taft Pleasant

CONTENTS

Endorsements.. i

Foreword... xii

Acknowledgements...xiv

Introduction..xviii

  1 Gifts From God 1

  2 Knew Them In The Womb 4

  3 The Light 7

  4 Show Your Love 10

  5 Respect And Manners 15

  6 It Takes A Village 19

  7 Grandparents 23

  8 Aunts And Uncles 26

  9 Boys... 30

10 Girls 33

11 In The Womb 37

12 Infants 40

13 Toddlers.. 43

14 Elementary School.. 46

15 Middle School 54

16 High School 57

17 College 61

18 Adult Children 64

19 Siblings... 68

20 Friends.. 72

21 Bullying.. 76

22 Mental Health 79

23 Church 82

24 Social Media 85

25 Holiday Traditions 88

26 The Painting 91

27 Pray Without Ceasing... 94

28 Mothers Determined To Pray................................. 96

Appendix.. 100

FOREWORD

My life has been committed to the improvement and growth in other peoples' lives since I was 16 years old. I get authentic joy when I see others reach their goals and have their dreams fulfilled. And the closer I am to the individual who achieves personal accomplishments, the more joy I realize.

Therefore, since no one is closer to me than my wife of 35 years, I have experienced unprecedented and unmatched joy from the completion of Donna's book, *"O Lord! Reflections of a Praying Mother."* Her strenuous labor that she invested into the completion of this book was only surpassed by the intense labor that she endured to bear the children whose lives became the basis of the book itself.

Because of my work and tremendously busy schedule that I have maintained through the years, Donna has been the parent that has had to be more than a basic mom to Malcolm and Martin. She has been more of a supermom - from waking them up every morning, driving them to school every day from pre-school through ninth grade, coordinating their clothes, driving them to and from basketball practice, helping them with homework, cooking their meals and screening their friends. And she prayed with them every single day until they left home to attend college.

Donna's superlative motherhood has earned her whatever accolades a great mother can receive. To manage the plethora of her motherly responsibilities while having to handle the dynamics of being my wife and the First Lady of a growing church may qualify her for a Nobel prize or MacArthur genius award. But it has been her prayer life and relationship with Jesus that have equipped her with the strength and wisdom she has needed to achieve phenomenal outcomes including the writing of this book.

This book is the narrative of a praying mother but the content is good for anyone. I am proud to be married to such a great woman who is easy to love and whose voice is finally being heard throughout the world.

DeForest B. Soaries, Jr.
Donna Soaries' husband

ACKNOWLEDGEMENTS

To the Almighty God that has made me everything I am and loved me through everything I'm not. This book is not something I ever thought I could accomplish. There are not words to express what God has done in my life. If I had one hundred and ten thousand tongues, I couldn't thank Him enough!

I am thankful for my husband and pastor, Rev. Dr. DeForest B. Soaries, Jr., for setting a standard of excellence for writing and giving thought to what you sow into others. Thank you for being the example of a hard worker that works to make other lives better. You have not just done this for your family. I believe for years to come our sons will hear of the seeds that you have sown. Soaries, I love you.

To my sons, Malcolm and Martin, I pray in years to come you will always know how special you are to me. I know I am a better person because I was blessed to be a mom and especially your mom! You are handsome, brilliant, funny and beautiful gifts that God gave to your dad and me.

To my "daughter" Tasha. I know I did not give birth to you, nor did I have to raise you or even pay for college, but I am grateful for the opportunity to have a "daughter" in you.

To my mother and father who showed me what it was to do what you do with excellence. Be kind to people and never purposely try to do things that hurt or embarrass people. Your love for God, people, giving and even cooking was passed down to my siblings and me.

To my twin brother, William Alfred Pleasant, who is one of the finest persons I know. Your life of integrity and love for others makes me so proud to have you as my twin brother. Your caring and giving to others are from the traditions of our parents, Edith and Taft Pleasant.

To my sisters, Velda Theresa Glover and Gertrude Elizabeth Spann, who have been examples of wonderful mothers. They not only had to be mother figures for my brother and me growing up, but they have been wonderful grandmothers. My siblings and I all enjoy laughing and making others laugh. We are all great cooks. Thanks Mom and Dad.

To Rev. Kathy Smallwood Johnson who spoke to me that there are two books in me. I thank you for always consistently checking on me with a prayer or a scripture to encourage me. I am not surprised they always come at the right times.

Dee Marshall, thank you for contributing to the vision of "Mothers Determined To Pray."

Thank you Rev. Dr. Melinda Contreras Byrd, Minister Faye Ralph and Toby Hemingway who have listened, supported me and prayed since my sons were very young.

Thank you to my mother-in-law, Mrs. Mitzi Soaries, Mom Sherman, and all the mothers/sister girlfriends that have prayed for me and prayed for my family over the years.

Thank you, Mom Anderson, for your support with my mom and for me as a mom.

Thank you to Rev. Grover C. Willcox and Helen Willcox, and the ministry of Conquerors Club. My life was saved and reborn through this ministry.

Thank you to Leanora Cousins who contributed to the editing of this book. What a great friend, mother, teacher and editor you are.

Sister Linda Brown, thank you for your prayers and texts with a word from the Lord every day. Sister Terry S. Whigham you are an amazing mother. Thank you for your devotions that you texted every day to encourage me.

Thank you Honey Sterzer! Never really knew I had so much going for me. God sent you into my life for this season of my life! What a wonderful woman you are!

Thank you to my First Baptist Church of Lincoln Gardens family! Thank you to all the Women's Retreat Committee members I have worked with over the years. You have enabled me to use the gifts and talents that God gave to me to contribute as First Lady.

Thank you to the "Mothers Determined To Pray" Mothers Council; Rev. Dr. Sheila Gipson, Deaconess Sandra Hayes, Leanora Cousins, Suzanne Hayes, Deaconess Robin Jackson and Linda Darby. Thank you to the prayer warriors, Minister Faye Ralph, Rev. Kathy Smallwood Johnson and Rev. Antonia Winstead. You have listening ears, you have prayed and provided unwavering support through the years.

First, I thank God through Jesus Christ for all of you because your faith is being reported all over the world. Romans 1:8 (NIV)

INTRODUCTION

When I decided to share some thoughts about being a mother in this book, I was excited and nervous at the same time. I kept thinking, *O Lord!* I find that I say these two words quite often. Sometimes it is a serious cry out to the Lord. Sometimes it is in response to something someone is telling me that is unbelievable, and sometimes it is just a response to something just plain funny. What I love about it is that my husband and my sons use it in response to each other. Sometimes in person or sometimes in a text message. It could be just in response to the fact that I made spaghetti for dinner which is one of their favorite meals! *O Lord!* This book is not intended to advise parents on what to do and what not to do when it comes to parenting. This book shares funny and serious stories about my sons and my life as a child, and as a mother. I have received a lot of advice over the years. Some solicited and some unsolicited. Some things have worked, and some would not work at all based on my situation. I think we have to be so careful in offering advice.

This thing called "parenting" does not come with a manual. The owner's manual for life for us is the Bible. We then have to apply it to our personal lives. No one can stop us from praying and so sometimes that's the best thing we can do. How great it would be if our children were prayed for as much as they were talked about!!

When I got married, I couldn't wait to have children. I come from a family that not only loved the children in our family but loved children in other families. Children make me laugh. I love hearing their funny stories. Of course, some stories make me laugh that may not make their parents laugh.

When I talk to others, my testimony has always been that I had a wonderful childhood. I had two parents that loved me, and I loved them. We had wonderful times together and I remember happy times. Every child does not have that story. As parents, we need to work hard on making it their story. This won't be easy, because life is not that simple. You have to work at it. We have no idea what is heading our way, but it is heading our way. At my local grocery store, there is a robot that moves around with a sensor that identifies when there are spills on the floor. You hear it beeping. Beep, beep, beep and then all of a sudden you will hear over the loudspeaker, "clean up needed in aisle 4." Wouldn't it be nice to have something that beeps and lets us know that something is heading our way with our children!?! Well, let me tell you this, it's coming! *O Lord!* Every age and every phase of their lives…a spill is coming. It could be in kindergarten when you take them to school on the first day. It could be in middle school when they are being bullied. It can be in high school when they don't make the football or cheerleading team. Their first heartbreak, their first college or job rejection. When your child becomes a parent and their child is going through life's journeys. You now need a next generation robot!

My mother was a great mother. As you already know, she was not a perfect mother, but she was a great mother. She built her children up with positive words. My sisters are wonderful mothers, not perfect, but in my eyes, wonderful. I can say I am a wonderful mother, not perfect, but wonderful.

Ten years ago, I founded the *"Mothers Determined To Pray"* Prayer Call. The prayer call was originally designed for mothers to come together to pray for our children for 15 minutes on a Saturday morning before we start a busy day of activities. The prayer is led by me or a prayer warrior from my circle of wonderful mothers.

The prayer call has now evolved into a ministry and a time in which we pray for mothers, children, families, the nation, the world, and we praise God for answered prayer. Please join us...

Mothers Determined To Pray
Saturday Mornings, 8:00am - 8:15am EST
712-432-0075 Access Code 311966#
Go to www.motherspray.com for prayer requests, praise reports, and testimonials...or to just stay in touch.

GIFTS FROM GOD

Gift; a thing given willingly to someone without payment; a present.[1] (Merriam-Webster Dictionary)

Psalm 127:3 (KJV) says, "children are a heritage for the Lord, offspring a reward from him and the fruit of the womb is His reward." The Message Translation says, "Don't you see they are God's best gift? The fruit of the womb is His generous legacy?

I started writing this book on November 1, which is my twin sons' birthday. When they were infants, I remember many people saying to me that I should enjoy every moment because the time will go so quickly and before you know it, they will be grown up! That didn't seem possible to me then. WOW!! Where did the time go?!

I remember the night I went to the hospital like it was yesterday. I had no idea what was ahead for me as a mother. The laughter, the tears, the hopes, the fears, but I would not change having them! Twelve hours of labor wasn't as bad as what some moms go through. One weighed 7lbs, and the other weighed 7lbs, 4 oz! *O Lord!* Needless to say, I had to have a Cesarean section. I came home seven days later to a beautifully decorated house by friends and family…and then began the journey. Sleep deprivation was just painful. I remember crying at the drop of a hat. The Federal Express carrier rang the doorbell and when he asked, "is your last name Soaries?" I just started crying! So funny now, but not funny then.

As you reflect on the first day with your child, I know you could not imagine what would be ahead. No matter what their age, you still do not know what is ahead. This I do know…God is with you and your child. During some of our challenging times as a mother, we don't always see them as "rewards." Think about the times when you get a gift. Beautifully wrapped, you hate to even open it. You are excited to see what the gift is. You carefully unwrap it, oh my goodness, this is beautiful, it looks and feels so good. It's beautiful! How did the giver know that this is such a perfect gift for me? I've been wanting and hoping for this for some time or you think what in the world is this? This is not what I asked for. What makes the giver think that I would like this? You say to yourself; I can't wait to regift this to someone else who may want this gift.

We say to ourselves they can't be gifts from God! If we are really honest, there may be times when we want to exchange that gift or even give it back! And think about this, at times, your child may have wanted to exchange or give back their parents if they could! Hold on, God is with you!! God hears and answers prayers. We have our journeys in life and so do our children. Thank God for them. They are a heritage from the Lord. Encourage and remind other parents who may reach out to you regarding challenges with their children, that they are "gifts." They may not want to hear it at the time, but the Word of God can't be disputed.

Children are a heritage from the LORD, offspring a reward from Him. Psalm 127:3 (NIV)

Children are a gift from the Lord; they are a real blessing. Psalm 127:3 (GNT)

Prayer: Thank you Lord for my precious gift. Thank you for choosing me as a parent for them. Help me in everything I do to be an example of what your love is. Thank you for the gift.

Assignment

Give your child a small gift today. Whether you can give it to them personally or you have to mail it. Put a note with it that says you want to give them a gift because you were reminded that they are a gift to you from the Lord!

2
KNEW THEM IN THE WOMB

"You made all the delicate, inner parts of my body and knit them together in my mother's womb." Psalm 139:13 (TLB)

There are times when I wonder if the Lord really knows what I'm going through. Actually, I know that He knows, but does He really understand how it affects me? I can get in those places when my heart is heavy regarding something with my child. The idiom, "tug at one's heartstrings," seems to apply so often to our children. When they tug at our hearts, it can be the greatest joy and the greatest hurt. When we cry or lament and worry, we cry out to the Lord, do you really understand?

Psalm 139 helps me so much with this. He knew me and He knew my children in the womb. As a matter of fact, He knew us before we were in the womb! Genesis 1 says that God created the earth when there was nothing. Verse 2 says the earth was formless and empty. That confirms for me that God knew us even before we were in our mother's womb. David reminds us how well God knows us. He knows us when we sit and rise. He knows our thoughts before they are in our minds. He knows words before we speak them. Because the Lord knows us so well, He knows all our ways. *Psalm 139:3 (MT).* I use this scripture to remind me to be completely honest when I am praying about a situation. I let Him know how hurt I am, how angry I am and when I just don't know what to do. Children can look to us to know everything and fix everything. *O Lord!* We then put the pressure on ourselves to be everything. Not only is it necessary to remind ourselves that we don't have all the answers, but sometimes, it's good to remind our children of just that. This reinforces for them that God knows about it and knows what to do about it.

My sons played basketball in school. In middle school, they both tried out for the team and only one made it. They were both really good at basketball. Even the one that did make the team couldn't figure out how he made it and his brother didn't. That was a hard weekend for our family. My son was in pain, his twin brother was in pain, and my husband and I were in pain. There is nothing worse than seeing your child hurt or sad. The author, Nicole Helget wrote, "a parent is only as happy as their saddest child."[2] We were angry with the coach, but we didn't take it out on him even though we wanted to. The coach told us later that even his wife told him that he had made a terrible decision. I just wanted to fix it. What did happen is that I showed a lot of love to my son. I would even go out to the basketball court and shoot around with him. At the time, I knew nothing about playing basketball, but I got on the court and kept rebounding the ball. A couple of days later, my son came home and told us that the coach made him honorary manager of the team. That meant he could travel with the team, sit on the bench, but he was told he was not to carry equipment, he was a manager. This helped all of us. The following year he made the team and tied the record for the highest scorer in the school! He was really supposed to be on that team. Things may not work out the way we want them to, but I am always reminded that God does know.

Prayer: God, things may be so heavy for me and I may wonder if you really understand, but please forgive me because I know that you do. You knew me before I was even a thought. I will trust you and I will trust your timing.

Assignment

On their birthday, write a note to your child sharing the experiences you had when they were in your womb. No complaining about how miserable you were in labor, just the fun things. Talk about what your cravings were. Talk about how they moved in the womb! If you were blessed to receive your child another way, talk about the day they came to you. They may think it's weird for you to reflect on that, but some children may enjoy knowing about it.

THE LIGHT

"This is the message we have heard from Him and declare to you: God is light; in Him there is no darkness at all. I John 1:5 (NIV)

I am a firm believer in speaking affirmations into my children. When my sons were young, a dear friend, Rev. Kathy Smallwood Johnson, told me to keep reminding them of how brilliant they are. One of her daughters has a doctorate in philosophy and the other daughter is a medical doctor. I believed her when she told me to speak brilliance into my sons.

Here's the thing, my sons are brilliant. I have been amazed since they were very young how smart they are. I don't just speak to things in their lives regarding intellect, but I remind them of things in their character. They both are such caring individuals. They are funny and respectful! I am now moving to remind them of the light that is within them. They gave their lives to the Lord early on. Now that Christ lives in them, the light of Christ is in them! Your child is brilliant. If they have given their lives to Christ, the light is in them. Remind them of that and speak that into them!

When I was growing up, gangs were not a threat to us. We heard about them, but they were not popular, and you did not seek them out. We now live in times where gangs are everywhere.

One of my son's favorite color was blue growing up and the other son wore red. There was no rhyme or reason to it other than they are identical twins. and it helped everyone and their parents sometimes to tell them apart. People that had a problem telling them apart as identical twins always looked for the colors to help them. We would give them that hint, but then they had to remember which color was assigned to which twin. *O Lord!* There came a time when I had to change colors all together. I realized that they could be identified as being a part of a gang just by wearing blue or red. Why are children attracted to gangs? Yes, there can be peer pressure to the extent that our children do it just because someone else is doing it, but for many it is a sense of belonging. Being connected with a group, being praised and supported, affirmed for even doing something wrong.

So often young people join gangs because they don't get enough affirmation from the unit called family. We get so busy that we don't think it's necessary to say "I love you" often. In years to come, I want my sons to always remember that their mom told them, as well as, showed them how much I loved them, and I did it on a frequent basis. Keep reminding your children about that light that is available to them. It is a strong light. There is no darkness at all! Jesus is the light!

"This little light of mine
I'm gonna let it shine
Let it shine, let it shine, let it shine..." [3]

Prayer: Lord, thank you for the light in me because of you. Help me to do whatever I can to ensure my children understand that they possess the same light!

Assignment

Give your child a tiny flashlight. Be creative, find one that is their favorite color! Ask them to always keep it. Even if it gets dusty or they don't know where it is, just tell them that it was given to them to remind them of the light that is in them!

4
SHOW YOUR LOVE

Whoever does not love does not know God, because God is love. 1 John 4:8 (NIV)

I love to surprise people with gifts for no special occasion. I will take a fruit basket to my hair salon. I have brought cinnamon buns to the staff at my doctor's office and lunch to owners of my dry cleaners as a Christmas gift. I really enjoy making Christmas wreaths personalized according to the person's name or hobby. I sometimes gave it to them in July, so they were really surprised it was for Christmas. I have taken dinner to families at church so that when they get home they can just relax and eat. I don't tell others what I'm doing; sometimes not even my husband. I feel funny even mentioning it in this book. My children often have to help me put these surprises together or load them up in the car. Why do I even like doing things like this? I realized it's because my parents did it! We often say that what others see you doing, speaks louder than what you say.

Recently, someone who works for one of my service providers, called and needed to talk to me for just 10 minutes. This young Latino lady has always had such a sweet personality. She told me that her heart was heavy because her relationship with her adult daughter was a strained one and had been so for a while. She felt that the answer was she needed to go to church. She had her reasons for not going to church that often, but she knew enough to want to connect more with God. She decided that she wanted to visit our church. As she was talking, I was praying that I could possibly find a church in our area that had services in Spanish so she could fully understand the service. Of course, I invited her to our service and asked her to let me know when she was coming so she could sit with me. I was just blessed by her desire to be somewhere in church to worship. Here is what is a little disconcerting. What if I had been nothing but a grouch every time I went to the business? What if I never asked how she is doing or how her family is doing? What if I always wanted to share the latest gossip with her? What if my language was less than flattering for someone who professed to be a child of God? What if I told dirty jokes from time to time? *O Lord!* I have been a customer of this service provider for over 10 years. It took over 10 years for this young lady to be in a place in her life where she had a need and she knew the need was the Lord.

The work and the witness are not over. The young lady came to church and joined the church the very first Sunday that she attended. She accepted Jesus Christ as her Lord and Savior and was baptized. She is at the point in her life that she wants to do everything that she possibly can do to please God. Now the real work begins. I can't get so busy that I am not in tune with what she needs to walk this walk. English is her second language and even though I told her that I would help her look for a church where her first language was spoken, she decided that she wanted to be at my church. There are female leaders in my church who speak Spanish and have befriended her and minister to her. Now I even pray that she will continue to feel the love at my church that I know we show.

Let your children see and participate in doing things for others… just because. Chances are they will also do it as adults. Teach them to show their love. I encourage you to look at I Corinthians 13(TLB) in the translation you prefer. I have provided the scripture from The Living Bible below:

13 If I had the gift of being able to speak in other languages without learning them and could speak in every language there is in all of heaven and earth, but didn't love others, I would only be making noise. ² If I had the gift of prophecy and knew all about what is going to happen in the future, knew everything about everything, but didn't love others, what good would it do? Even if I had the gift of faith so that I could speak to a mountain and make it move, I would still be worth nothing at all without love. ³ If I gave everything I have to poor people, and if I were burned alive for preaching the Gospel but didn't love others, it would be of no value whatever.

⁴ Love is very patient and kind, never jealous or envious, never boastful or proud, ⁵ never haughty or selfish or rude. Love does not demand its own way. It is not irritable or touchy. It does not hold grudges and will hardly even notice when others do it wrong. ⁶ It is never glad about injustice but rejoices whenever truth wins out. ⁷ If you love someone, you will be loyal to him no matter what the cost. You will always believe in him, always expect the best of him, and always stand your ground in defending him. [8] All the special gifts and powers from God will someday come to an end, but love goes on forever. Someday prophecy and speaking in unknown languages and special knowledge—these gifts will disappear. [9] Now we know so little, even with our special gifts, and the preaching of those most gifted is still so poor. [10] But when we have been made perfect and complete, then the need for these inadequate special gifts will come to an end, and they will disappear.

[11] It's like this: when I was a child I spoke and thought and reasoned as a child does. But when I became a man(woman) my thoughts grew far beyond those of my childhood, and now I have put away the childish things. [12] In the same way, we can see and understand only a little about God now, as if we were peering at his reflection in a poor mirror; but someday we are going to see him in his completeness, face-to-face. Now all that I know is hazy and blurred, but then I will see everything clearly, just as clearly as God sees into my heart right now. [13] There are three things that remain—faith, hope, and love—and the greatest of these is love.

Prayer: God, we have been told to be witnesses to men and women. Sometimes we get so busy that we think that others are supposed to do that because we have other things to do. I am so grateful that someone witnessed to me, and I pray that you will use me as an example for my children that we are responsible for souls that need to be saved and delivered.

Assignment

Tell someone about your love for God today. It may be the person that does your hair, the cashier at the supermarket or just invite them to your church. Don't be surprised by what the Lord will do.

RESPECT AND MANNERS

God created us a little lower than the angels. Psalms 8:5/Hebrews 2:7 (NIV)

How amazing is that? God created us a little lower than the angels! Even though we always want to be in a place of humility, knowing this makes you want to stick out your chest and put pep in your step! While growing up, it was always emphasized to be respectful to our elders. Being from the South, we always had to address those older than us as Mr., Mrs., or Miss. We answered, "yes ma'am" and "no sir." Never ever were we allowed to call them by their first name. You were almost afraid to call a person by their first name for fear that lightening would strike! Not really, but your fear of what your parents might do kept you in check. As a parent, I take great pleasure in hearing my children address an older person with some kind of title. Some adults don't mind being called by their first name and they will give permission to my sons to do so. One of my sons is a basketball coach, and some of his younger parents tell him that he doesn't have to address them by their last names. He will comply only when he is given permission.

Recently, I was at a drive-thru to get some soup and a sandwich. After I placed my order, I pulled up to the window to pay and after the young lady gave me my total and I gave her my money, she said, "thank you honey." *O Lord!* I was taken back and then even more taken back when she gave me my food and my change, she said "have a good day honey." I must admit I was appalled. She looked as if she was in her 20's calling an older woman "honey!" It really stayed on my mind. The next time I went to that drive-thru, the same young lady was there and called me "honey" again, and so I decided to ask her age. She said she was about to turn 30. But wait, one evening, my husband called me to say that he would pick up a quick bite on his way to an event. I suggested he get soup from the same drive-thru. As he drove away, he called me from the car and said, "Donna, the young girl at the window called me "honey!"…but this was a different young lady! When it happened to me, I didn't feel the need to correct her or embarrass her because I didn't feel she was being disrespectful. She was obviously raised differently. I also believe she was not trained to call customers "honey," but it felt so strange.

Here's the key, children do what they are taught or what they observe. My sons have never heard me use any obscenities. It is because I don't curse. I never have. One time I was so angry at someone I spelled the curse word out loud for them to hear. That's a mess! *O Lord!* I encourage you to instill in children the need to respect their elders. Say "please" and "thank you." Speak up when you are speaking to someone and look them in the eye. When shaking a person's hand, give a firm handshake. We were taught to do this when we were growing up. We play a big part in creating a better more respectful society by what we pour into our children.

This funny story comes to mind about my dad. When I was little, our small church was instructed to merge with another small church in our denomination. I remember speaking to a man in the choir from the other church and reaching out to shake his hand. He squeezed my hand so tight it actually hurt and put a tear in my eye! While driving home, I told my dad what happened. The next time we were at choir rehearsal, I knew I was going to avoid this gentleman even though he seemed to be very nice. At the next choir rehearsal, I heard my dad say hello and call the gentleman's name as he reached out to shake his hand. I watched to see if my dad looked uncomfortable from the handshake. Much to my surprise, I saw the gentleman say hello and while shaking my dad's hand, he went up on his toes and the pitch of his voice went up an octave! My dad smiled as only my dad could smile, and I felt like I could hear him thinking that will teach you to squeeze my daughter's hand that way again! Oh, how I loved my dad!

I was in a restroom at the airport recently and after I washed my hands, I used the automated dryer. When the loud air sound ended, I heard an automated voice say, "thank you so much for washing your hands." Wow, have we come to that?! We have to be thanked for washing our hands by a robot?! When we feel confident in who we are and whose we are, it doesn't bother us to be respectful of others. We are created a little lower than the angels.

Prayer: Lord please help me to be consistent with how I show respect for others so that my children desire to be respectful. Help me to be conscience of it so that it will become the norm on my job, at church and in my home…I want to live it.

Assignment

Spend a day making sure that you are thanking those that deserved to be thanked! Sometimes you may not think they really need it, but it can really do something for a person's attitude and their day.

6

IT TAKES A VILLAGE

"From eternity to eternity I am God. No one can snatch anyone out of my hand. No one can undo what I have done." Isaiah 43:13 (NLT)

"It takes a whole village to raise a child is an African proverb that means that an entire community of people must interact with children for those children to experience and grow in a safe and healthy environment. The villagers look out for the children. This does not mean an entire village is responsible for raising a child or the children of a crowd."[4]

The coach of the women's basketball team at the university near our church is a member of our church. For many years, my husband and I invited members of the team to our home for home-cooked meals and a home away from home to relax, watch movies, or do schoolwork. As they would also play basketball with our sons, it was a "win, win" situation for everyone. My husband and I became a part of the village for these young ladies. My sons were very young, but even then, I hoped that when my sons go off to college, someone would look out for them and invite them to have a safe haven away from home. Sometimes team members were not able to go home on holidays because of scheduling of games, and they knew that our home was available for food, fun, fellowship and rest. They respected my husband and often times someone would look to him regarding spiritual counsel. My husband also talked to them about basketball, but I think they were just being polite and listened. They knew who their real coach was!

One young lady came over more often than others and she became like a daughter. I finally had the opportunity to share some words of wisdom that I had saved up in case I ever had a girl. What a joy it was for me! We talked about relationships. We went shopping together for clothes, makeup, etc. We talked about basketball (by now, I was pretty knowledgeable about basketball). It was just nice spending time with her. I constantly reminded her of what a great job her mother and father had done raising her. She was very smart, respectful and funny. She was even a trusted babysitter. She was also an amazing point guard. Michael Jordan, this young lady, and my sons are the reasons that I fell in love with basketball. My sons referred to her then and to this day as their sister. One night, my husband and I went to a parent teacher conference and the teacher said to us, "Mr. and Mrs. Soaries, we did not know that you had a daughter." *O Lord!* The teacher told us that our sons make reference to their "sister" all the time!

This "daughter" called me the night she got engaged! I had the pleasure of singing at the wedding and was around for the birth of her two daughters. Although her children have two wonderful biological grandmothers and grandfathers, I love them all even though we are not related. The girls call me "grandma" and my husband, "grandpa," and my sons, "uncle." Even though this "daughter" and her family now live in another part of the country, I am so happy to still be part of their village. We talk or "FaceTime" at least once a week. My sons tease her husband, to this day, that he only got to marry her because they approved of him, barely.

We are always reminded of the African proverb, "it takes a village…" Some may call it mentoring, but consider focusing, following and pouring into a child for years to come. Be a cheerleader, a shoulder to cry on, an advisor, a prayer partner and don't forget financial support, if needed. Tasha lived with us while she earned her masters' degree. She tried out for the WNBA, she was an assistant basketball coach at three universities and is now a head coach at a Division 1 university! We couldn't be prouder of her. I didn't have any labor pains, go through puberty struggles or pay for college, but we have an amazing adopted daughter, son-in-law and two granddaughters!

Just remember this…while you are helping others in the village, there may be times you will need someone in the village to help you with yours. I know that it has happened many times that we were grateful for the village. For years to come, we will always be grateful for the village.

Prayer: Lord, direct me to some child outside of my family that just may need a little extra from someone. Direct me as to what to do and when to do it. It may just mean praying for them on a consistent basis over the years. Help me to be consistent. Help me to make a difference in their life.

Assignment

Identify who is in your village. Stay connected to your village. Let them know they are a part of the village and pray for them when they come to mind.

7
GRANDPARENTS

I am reminded of your sincere faith, which first lived in your grand-
mother Lois and in your mother Eunice and, I am persuaded, now
lives in you also." 2 Timothy 1:5 (NIV)

I was not fortunate enough to know either of my grandparents. Both my maternal and paternal grandparents passed away
before I was born. My mother and father often said they just
wished that their parents would have known that they had twins.
Grandparents, if they use their God-given wisdom, get a second
chance to do things better than they had done raising their own
children. My husband is a pastor, and on the Sundays that baby
blessings are done, he always reminds us that grandparents' job is
to spoil the grandchildren! Let them do everything they wouldn't
let their own children do and then send them home!

Grandparents are living longer. Sometimes it is because they
became grandparents younger. At any rate, on my Saturday morning prayer calls, I often pray for grandparents to be alert to what
their grandchildren are exposed to. Social media exposes our children to things that most grandparents did not have to consider
when their children were growing up. I often think of what my
parents would have done or thought to be able to make a call on
a phone that was not attached to the wall and see their grandchildren on a screen! They would be amazed by the way children

dress and even the way children speak. I wish I would have tried to speak to my parents using incorrect grammar purposely! That dialogue would not have had a chance to survive!

When we were growing up, we automatically went to church on Sunday. We got our clothes ready and our shoes shined on Saturday night. We have generations of children that just don't go to church. Imagine what this must feel like for a grandparent. They pray for the souls of their grandchildren. What will become of them? This is a generation that doesn't know what it feels like to be in Sunday school every Sunday, to learn a part in the Easter and Christmas play, and to sing in the children's choir.

My sons are blessed to have their paternal grandmother living. They enjoy so much laughing with her mainly because she is so funny even though she doesn't know it sometimes. Their grandmother, "Gammy," adores them and prays for them. They did get to know my mother up until their high school years. They were too young to remember a lot of things about my father before he passed. Their paternal grandfather passed away before they were born. My husband and I have told them stories about both of their grandfathers. It is so important to share the jewels of their heritage. I am blessed to have two "adopted" granddaughters. I love them so much. I pray for them and remind them of the greatness that is in them. I love how they make me laugh even when others may not think it's funny!

No matter what, grandparents have the indelible job to pray for their grandchildren. There is something about a grandparent praying that is powerful. Maybe because they have a good idea of what's ahead and even if they don't know specifically, they know that prayer is what they need. To my dismay, my sons got tattoos when they were in college. *O Lord!* One son has two tattoos, "Dubois," which is his middle name, and the other tattoo is "I am a performer, Life is a stage." The other son got a tattoo with the names of all of his grandparents! WOW! It could have been worse!

I see my dad in my sons and that makes me smile. He was an English teacher, a school principal, and a trustee in his church. I was told that their paternal grandfather was a disciplinarian. I did not have the pleasure of meeting him, but I know he was revered, by many, as a Pastor, as an educator, and he was a high school vice principal. Although their maternal grandmother is deceased, both grandmothers are women of class and elegance. They both were also educators with giving caring hearts. My sons come from a family heritage that consists of intelligent, highly educated, spiritual people.

Assignment

If your child's grandparents are living, have them arrange to interview their grandparents. Make an appointment to do it and be very creative with it. Have questions arranged in advance to learn more about their grandparents and consider making some kind of book or even video if they choose. If grandparents are deceased, encourage them to do some kind of research.

8
AUNTS AND UNCLES

Mordecai had a cousin named Hadassah, whom he had brought up because she had neither father nor mother. This young woman, who was also known as Ester, had a lovely figure and was beautiful. Mordecai had taken her as his own daughter when her father and mother died. Esther 2:7 (NIV)

When we were growing up, we had "uncles" and "aunts" whom we were not related to by blood. We did not always know that they weren't related, and this went on for years. Some of the things they would do for us and with us just felt like family. They would babysit us or take us to our favorite fun places. They gave us our favorite foods and snacks when we visited with them. They had things in common with our parents. They loved the Lord, they liked to laugh. We did not hear them using curse words in their conversation because our parents did not use curse words in their conversation. In addition to that, they could reprimand us if they needed to. They had standards and lifestyles like our parents. They loved God just as my parents loved God.

Before I knew it, I was the actual aunt of 11 nieces and nephews. One of my sisters had six children and one had five. I loved them all. I often wish I had been a more attentive aunt to them. I have had regrets that I was not a better Aunt. I have asked for God's forgiveness, but even after I had my own children, I wish that I had communicated more with them. I wish I had consistently shared the love of Jesus with them more, but I do pray for them now and ask the Lord to lead them in their lives.

We have to be careful about who we introduce to our children to have them attached enough and secure enough to call them aunt or uncle. It may sound cute, but what they need to know is that we want them to relate to that person as a relative, then they should be able to trust them under any circumstance. We also need our children to know that no matter how close they are, these people are not allowed to do anything to them that would harm them. There are disturbing high risks of children being abused by someone they thought they could trust. *O Lord!*

My sons have "aunts" and "uncles" who are not blood related and they still call them aunt and uncle; Aunt Melinda, Uncle Vernon, Uncle Donnie, Aunt Phyllis, Aunt Sandra, Uncle Gerald, Aunt Kim, Aunt Malinda, Uncle Bill, Aunt Ellen, Uncle Bob, Aunt Cindy, Uncle Ron, Aunt Sharon, Uncle Zed. When my husband became Pastor of our church, we were blessed to meet a couple who were a deacon and deaconess and soon became Aunt Faye and Uncle Stewart. They began watching our sons when they were toddlers. For the longest time the twins called Stewart "Uncle Neck." For quite some time, we could not figure out why until we realized that every time he saw them, he would hug them and kiss them on their necks. That is why they called him "Uncle Neck!" Throughout the years, Uncle Stewart would play basketball with them until late night and when they spent the weekend, the boys always looked forward to the ritual of ordering from Pizza Hut on Friday nights. Faye and Stewart loved our sons as if they were their own. Then there was Aunt Toby and Uncle Dickie. Their son was a year younger than our sons. My boys were always coming up with creative ways to get to their house on Sunday afternoon after church like complimenting Aunt Toby on her hair! My sons still refer to them as Aunt Toby and Uncle Dickie. Both aunts and uncles pray for my children to this day. My sons, Malcolm and Martin are now known as "uncle" to two little girls who are now part of our family. They love their "nieces" and the girls love their "uncles."

Let's talk about "blood" aunts and uncles. My sons' aunts and uncles are amazing! They are at the age now where they don't reach out to their aunts and uncles a lot.(The truth is that they don't reach out to too many people a lot!) However, I do know they know that their aunts and uncles love them. What's most important to me is that they have aunts and uncles who pray for them on a regular basis. If they don't always send a birthday card or present, it means so much to me when I'm asked how they are doing and want to hear about what's going on in their lives. They want to know accomplishments, they want to hear funny stories, and they want to know if they are in a good place or not. Their aunts and uncles want to know what to pray for and even if they don't know specifically…they are still praying!

There is something about my sons' biological uncles that make them laugh. They love to hear funny stories. My brother, Uncle Bop, is funny, in general. Like our father, he likes to tell funny stories. My husband's brother, Uncle Craig, makes them laugh to the extent that when they are in his presence, or we say his name, they just start laughing! What I know for sure is that both of their uncles are prayer warriors and they cover my children in prayer. My sisters, Aunt Gert and Aunt Velda, pray for me, my husband and my sons. They ask about them whenever we talk. My husband's sister, Aunt Terri, was with me the first week my sons came home from the hospital. She covers them in prayer. My other sisters-in-law cover my sons in prayer too, and that would be Aunt Rochelle and Aunt Shirley. My best friends, Aunt Melinda and Aunt Faye, cover them in prayer. When I say "cover" in prayer, I mean pray for them consistently. As their mother, I am so grateful for aunts and uncles. I am grateful for their blood relatives and the adopted ones. I let them know (maybe not as often as I should) that I thank God for them. I thank God that they pray for my family. I thank God for their listening ear and their advice and support.

Prayer: Thank you Lord for aunts and uncles who have loved my children along with me. Thank you for the times they have prayed for my children, given them advice, and just been there as needed. Bless them for their sacrifices and their support.

Assignment

Send a fruit basket, some cookies, or just a note that says I appreciate what you have been as an aunt and uncle! I could not have made it without you.

9
BOYS

So in the course of time Hannah became pregnant and gave birth to a son. She named him Samuel, saying, "Because I asked the Lord for him." 1 Samuel 1:20 (NIV)

When I found out that I was pregnant, I was ecstatic! My husband prayed for twins and I prayed for boys. The Lord blessed us with identical twin boys! God answered both of our prayers! Some say that boys are easier than girls. Some say the opposite. There is no guarantee. What it all boils down to is that they will become infants, toddlers, young children, pre-teens, teenagers and they will be adults by the grace of God. As a parent, I will be responsible for teaching them how to respect people. We know there are all kinds of styles that are accepted, but if our boys never hear that you take your hat off when you are in a building they will be insulted when someone else says " take your hat off." My sons never participated in the "sagging" pants trend. I am so glad. I can't even imagine what my parents would have thought to see their grandchildren or any child for that matter walking around with their underwear showing on purpose! *O Lord!*

In case you have not noticed, it is a new day from when we grew up. I have a good relationship with my sons. We laugh a lot, and we talk a lot about various subjects. They both talk to me, of course, based on their particular interests. I know they don't tell me everything, but I didn't tell my parents everything. I know that my sons aren't excited about things I like to do, like decorating and some of the creative ideas I have for our house, but they like that I am happy doing these things.

When my sons were seniors in high school, I had their friends over once a month for some ice cream sundaes. They seemed to connect with my husband as he talked to them about goals and life in general. My son reported back to us that some of their friends took what they heard from my husband very seriously and were writing down goals, as well as, three and five-year plans. We did not do it as often as I would have liked, but you never know the impact it had. Even though my sons are not in touch with a lot of their high school friends, they have some friends that are wonderful adults.

I must say that in this time of our lives, I pray a lot for African-American males. We have to talk to them about how to treat women. Be respectful in the way you communicate with them. At the risk of being called chauvinistic, teach them how to open the car door for a woman and not walk in front of them when entering a building. We have talked to them about what to do and not do when pulled over by a police officer. Teach them not to have anything that might appear to be a weapon. Don't reach for anything, phone, your license, a pen. Don't reach for anything. Put your hands where they can be seen.

It has been said that boys are closer to their moms and girls are closer to their dads as the years go on. This could be in many instances, but you really can't generalize it. I just know that I have been blessed to have two sons!

Prayer: Lord, thank you for our sons. I pray for all boys, young men, adult men. Help me to let my sons know on a consistent basis how amazing they are because you created them. Protect them and keep them from dangers seen and unseen. Let them feel your love through us. Help us to affirm them with consistency. Help them to to be the men that you created them to be. Amen.

Assignment

Identify a boy in your life. It may be your own, a relative, or one of your children's friends. It could be a young boy in the choir at your church. Find out what their favorite snack is. Check with the parent first and give them an abundance of the snack. Write a note that tells them how great they are!

GIRLS

When the child grew older, she took him to Pharaoh's daughter and he became her son. She named him Moses, saying, "I drew him out of the water." Exodus 2:10 (NIV)

I don't have girls, but I am a girl. The saying that girls are sugar and spice and everything nice I thought applied to me coming up. My parents probably would have agreed that generally they described me that way. I was mild mannered, polite and respectful. Of course, there were exceptions. Hormones evolve, teenage years happen, and things change. I know there must have been times when my mother wondered, who is this person?! Since I did not have girls, I can only go by what others have shared and to remember how I was when I became a teenager. But it can be very challenging for a young girl to now think that she is an adult in the family. Rolling of eyes, sucking of teeth! Where does this come from?

When I was a teenager, I remember deciding that the next time my mother and I were having words back and forth that I was going to hum and then start singing. I was going to hum or sing something softly in order not to have an encounter with her that would not end well. What in the world made me think that humming or singing while my mother was talking to me would end well?! My older sister, Velda, was in the car when I put this plan into action. I could see my sister's shoulders moving and her head go down as she was laughing. I wish I had run it by her before I came up with this strategy. Thank God my mother was driving! I was in the back seat and all my mother could do was look at me in the rear-view mirror and say, "I know you are not humming while I'm talking to you!!" Where did I get that dumb idea from?!

I enjoyed dressing up, having pretty things and admiring pretty things. When I was a little girl, I remember there was a famous model who was a member of my church. Her name was Emily Miles. She was a model, and a noted hat designer and her mother, Rose Rollins, was on the Trustee Board of our church. As a young girl, I often looked for Ms. Miles in church. She always sat in the next to the last pew. You could not miss her. She was fabulous! She was right out of a Vogue or, should I say, Ebony Magazine, as far as I was concerned. We know that all things beautiful are not just admired by girls, but as a girl, I loved things that were beautiful. I had in my mind that when I grew up, I wanted to look fabulous and dress like Emily Miles. Later, I realized my mother was also a sharp dresser, and I wanted to emulate her also.

I know that peer pressure exists for males and females, but there seems to be something about girls in that they tend to worry more about what people think of them and say about them. It just seems like girls experience depression, self-medicating and eating disorders at a higher rate than boys. Why is that? It is imperative that our children know that that they are amazing. Our belief that we were created a little lower than the angels is not just a cliché or saying, it is scripture, Hebrews 2:7. Psalm 139 says that, "we are fearfully and wonderfully made." It is the Word of God.

We struggle with our body images. Psalm 139 says that, He created our inward parts. Girls and boys need to be reminded of this, but I think especially girls. Sometimes I imagine God scratching His head. If He gives us curly hair, we want it straight. If our hair is straight, we find a way to make it curly. We want to enhance or reduce body parts. We want to be taller or shorter. We want our skin tone to be a different color. We don't embrace freckles, big or little noses. Millions of dollars are spent to change what we were born with. I think because we are not happy with how we look, there is a tendency to not affirm others. We see beautiful articles of clothing, jewelry, shoes or even hair, but we will not speak the words to compliment them. *O Lord!* What in the world is that about?

Try it, compliment someone and see how much better you feel. I know that even when we tell our children how amazing they are, one of their peers can cancel that all out. Just do your best to be consistent with affirmations!

Assignment

Identify a girl in your life. It may be your own, a relative, or one of your children's friends. It could be an usher at your church. Find out what their favorite snack is. Check with the parent first and give them an abundance of the snack. Write a note that tells them how great they are!

11

IN THE WOMB

For you created my inmost being; you knit me together in my mother's womb. Psalm 139:13 (NIV)

One of the best gifts I received after I learned that I was expecting, was the book, "What to Expect When You're Expecting,"[5] by Heidi Murkoff. The author described what to expect in your body during every month of your pregnancy. I was constantly tempted to read ahead so I would know what was coming next.

The experience of a child growing inside of you has to be one of the most incredible feelings anyone can have. I loved it. I was so happy to be pregnant, even with the highs and lows. Many women experience morning sickness. I did not have one day of morning sickness. Some people say that you get morning sickness when you are expecting a girl, but as you already know, morning sickness can happen with either boys or girls, so that is not true. Indigestion comes with girls and boys. When I suffered with so much indigestion, I was told that the boys must have a lot of hair, and they did. Most women experience dramatic changes to their body. There is the swelling of the feet, hands, face, and of course, the stomach! There are sleepless nights and times when you can't eat and sleep and times when all you want to do is eat and sleep. I was the latter! *O Lord!*

Many women experience cravings. I didn't crave pickles and ice cream, but I ate all of the watermelon and tuna fish sandwiches available to me. We can use this time as an opportunity to feed our bodies with healthy items. Expectant mothers must focus on the fact that what we eat, our baby is consuming. We can use this as an opportunity to exercise, walk, do yoga, or just stretch. It would be wonderful if we could just use this new beginning for baby and mom to make life changes.

I had prayed that my children would not be born premature. That is often the case with multiple births. I imagined that it would be a little difficult managing twins and I was concerned about what to expect if I have "preemies." All of my nieces and nephews were big babies and my mom had told me that my oldest sister, Velda, was 9 lbs. and she was delivered at home! I was ten days overdue from my due date. After about two days beyond my due date, my doctor encouraged me to walk and she would schedule an induced labor. I remember walking to the end of my short but sloping driveway and promising God that if He got me back into the house, I would not leave the house until time to deliver my precious sons. I knew that my sons were going to be big babies just based on the fact that on every doctor's visit I got an update on their weight.

I finally went into labor 10 days after my due date. I called my doctor and she said to go right to the hospital. I was only in labor 12 hours, and my doctor wanted to know if the interns that were on staff could observe the delivery. I think in that state you just answer questions based on what you think will make things move faster. I was in so much pain at about 10am my doctor said let's give it one more hour and if I had not dilated more, she would do a C-section at 11am. I told my husband I didn't want to wait an hour because I was in so much pain and he encouraged me that since I loved and trusted my doctor that we should wait. I then did what I said I would never do in the delivery room. I turned on my husband. I reminded him that he was not the one in labor and he had no say so in this matter. I didn't want him holding my hand or even talking to me. So embarrassing!! On November 1, 1989 at 11:00am and 11:02 am, my sons were delivered by Caesarean section. They weighed 7 lbs. and 7 lbs. 4 oz. Yes, that's right, I was carrying almost 15 pounds!

Assignment

The next time someone you know has a baby, offer to do something helpful. I think a good hot meal is always welcomed soon after they arrive home. It may be nice to have something for the family the first week the baby comes home, but I promise you that a month after the baby has come home and all the hoopla has died down, they will welcome something. Just find out what that something is. Find out what they identify as helpful. You may be surprised what they request but hear them and believe them.

12
INFANTS

When Elizabeth heard Mary's greeting, the baby leaped in her womb, and Elizabeth was filled with the Holy Spirit. Luke 1:41 (NIV)

One of the many words of advice that are given to new moms is to sleep while the baby is sleeping so that they are not so worn out from night feedings. The draw back here is that you are not able to accomplish tasks when trying to sleep when the baby sleeps. Bottles have to be washed if you are not nursing, clothes have to be washed and you like to take a shower and brush your teeth before 4pm in the afternoon; and prayerfully, you have a child that is not colicky. My twins did not sleep at the same time for the longest time. As soon as one would fall asleep the other one would wake up.

My twins are identical. As infants we really could not tell them apart. My oldest twin has a birthmark behind his ear. Very often, we would check behind the ear of one of them to determine which son is which. I tried to breastfeed for five minutes. That's right, five minutes. The nurse kept encouraging me to just try, but first of all, it hurt. I had a C-section and since I was so uncomfortable, most of all, I needed someone to help me feed them. I told her to bring on the bottles. Friends and family could help with feeding times. It is such a precious time seeing them come into their own.

They start to recognize you. They smile every now and then, even though at first it could be gas.

When it is your first child, you tend to want to hold them all the time. I had the nerve to try to do that with the twins. I would rock one to sleep and then rock the other. I spent so much of my time putting them to sleep that before I knew it, they were awake already for their next feeding. My pediatrician must have recognized the look of sleep deprivation when she saw me at their office visits. For me, she suggested that when they go down for the night, make sure they are dry and full, kiss them, say "I love you," and let them cry. Guess who cried the most on the first night...I did! *O Lord!* When they finally plopped down in the crib (which they both did at the same time), I was exhausted, but it worked! It took just three nights for them to get used to this new routine. Someone told me to put on soft music when I put them down, and this would also be a signal that it is time to go to sleep. I had a tape of hymns that I used as accompaniment for my concerts (I forgot to mention that I'm a classical soprano) and it became something they loved. The great thing about it was that I could bring a tape with me when we traveled, and it helped me put them down to sleep no matter where they were.

There were a lot of people that wanted to help with the babies. That's a sensitive time for a first-time mom. You have to follow your mind. I preferred having support from people who did not complain about how much work was involved in caring for my babies or their own babies! Complaining is not something you want around you during this time. It is great to have help from people you are close to and who understand how to deliver unsolicited advice in a caring and sensitive manner. It is wonderful to get advice in the name of love.

Assignment

Please consider giving a basket of baby products or a gift card to the parents of a newborn three or four months *after* the baby is born. They will still need them and it will be greatly appreciated.

13
TODDLERS

"Out of the mouth of babes and sucklings hast thou ordained strength because of thine enemies, that thou mightiest still the enemy and the avenger." Psalms 8:2 (KJV)

Everyone tried to prepare me for the terrible twos. They told me if you can just make it through the twos, you'll be able to make it the rest of the way with some form of sanity. At age two, my twin sons were mild, docile, and listened to instructions all the time. I had decided that the Lord knew how hard it was going to be with twins, so I didn't have to experience the terrible twos! Then they turned three. It was like two tornadoes came through my house and my life for a whole year! *O Lord!* Something was always happening. They were learning new words. They were exploring more. I came in the kitchen one day and they had gotten into the pantry and had mixed pancake syrup with flour and smeared it on the kitchen floor. Of course, they smiled when I walked into the room, and I smiled, too. Another time, I had just finished bathing them, ran in their room to get their clothes, and that quick, returned to find them covered in baby powder such that you could only see their eyes! I enjoyed praying with them and saying grace with them over meals. Although they only said "Amen," they said it with much fervor and exhilaration at the end!

You have to watch toddlers constantly. They are exploring everything in sight. They are not trying to be defiant or a nuisance. In their minds, they are just doing what they are supposed to do. Children start walking, talking, and if you are blessed, getting potty trained! A lot of things happen in the life of a toddler, but the time moves quickly. Enjoy the time, the hugs and the kisses. You may get them without even being asked. This is the age when potty training begins. Let me tell you right now, it will happen. I got so concerned that potty training was taking so long that my sons would be at their weddings with their Pullups® on! They have all kinds of creative things now. However, we had just a simple video with songs for them to sing along saying, "potty, potty." They would stand in front of the TV, sing along with the video and go potty standing right there. They eventually got it and they were just toddlers. I often hear that girls potty train earlier, but just hang in there. They will get it. In case you don't remember, it took a lot of people a while to get it. Maybe even you.

When my sons were three, one son decided to walk away from us in an airport. My husband gave me a signal to just let him be so we could see how far he would go. He never looked back! My husband followed him for a good distance. People would look at this adorable little boy swinging his arm while he was walking and I'm sure wondering why he was by himself. When people would look back a few yards, they would see a man that looked just like him and assumed the little boy was ok. MY SON NEVER LOOKED BACK! It was as if he knew that if he needed his dad, he would be there.

Enjoy this stage. When they are older, you want them to walk on a path of confidence when they enter adulthood. You want them to keep walking and not look back. However, you do want them to have the assurance that when they need to look back for guidance or advice, they know you are there.

Fear thou not; for I am with thee; be not dismayed; for I am thy God; I will strengthen thee; yea I will help thee; yea I will uphold thee with the right hand of righteousness. Isaiah 41:10 (KJV)

Assignment

If your child is a toddler and you are trying to potty train, create your own song to sing every time they are successful or at least make the attempt. Wouldn't it be nice to sing it at their wedding as a tribute! *O Lord!*

14

ELEMENTARY SCHOOL

For you been my hope, Sovereign Lord, my confidence in my youth.
Psalm 71:5 (NIV)

Elementary school years were challenging and a bit rough for us as parents, but very memorable with a bit of humor sometimes. I don't think it was rough for our sons, more fun times for them. The following true stories all happened during the elementary school years.

When my sons were in kindergarten, we met with one of their teachers who told us that the recess monitors reported our sons for chasing another student and it seemed to be a problem. This was one of those many times when I was so grateful for my husband. He asked the question, "are they the only ones doing this?" The teacher could not answer the question because she was not outside with the students during recess. My husband asked if we could meet with the teachers who made the report, and we went right upstairs to the teacher's lounge to ask them directly. I have to admit I was astonished. Their answer was "no" they were not the only ones. I would have never thought to question that. The kindergarten teacher who reported that to us was embarrassed that she had even mentioned it to us. I took the opportunity to go to the school the next day and observe recess. Yes, my sons were playing and running like everyone else, and the young boy that they were chasing at times seemed to absolutely love it. They were having a great time during recess. When you receive a report from any teacher that you may not be happy about, take a deep breath and be ready to hear everything. There is no better feeling for a child to know that their parent is going to investigate, listen and get to the bottom of things. Innocent until proven otherwise.

One day the doorbell rang and when I opened the door, much to my surprise, it was a police officer. He asked me, "is everything all right?" because they received a 911 call from this address. No one had said anything, they hung up, but based on procedure he had to check. I immediately called my husband to see if he was ok because he was working in his office in the basement. He told us both he did not call. I then called both of my sons who were upstairs, they both ran down to us, and it appeared that they were fine and they stated that. I asked did either of them call 911. One son said, without reservation, he did not. The other son said, without reservation, he did. What!? I swallowed hard. My husband asked, "why did you call 911? This is very serious." He said, "I know. Police officers came to our school today and talked to us. They told us a lot of different things but the one thing I know they said was, if we ever need help, call 911. Mommy told me to clean up my room and I needed help!" *O Lord!*

A package was delivered with my husband's name on it. He opened it to find a $250 photo scanner. He said, "I never ordered this!" One of my sons answered, "I did, Dad." My husband said "how did you pay for it?" My son said, "I used the card on file." My husband said, "it's $250" and my son said, "plus tax." *O Lord!*

Our sons earned excellent grades in school, but this son was a perfectionist and took pride in getting A's on all tests. One night during a parent teacher conference, the teacher showed us a test this son had taken and there were several answers marked wrong with Xs. We were taken aback. What was going on?? My husband took a closer look at the test and realized the first answer that had been marked wrong was actually correct. My husband then checked the next answer and it was also correct. This was a test that was going to be on his record for the school year. My husband was so upset and so was I! He was so upset to the extent that he stood up and told the teacher that this was unacceptable. It didn't help matters any when the teacher told us that the children in the class had exchanged papers and corrected the tests. That meant that the teacher had not checked the tests and was about to record a grade that just was not true. My husband walked out of the class to go to, what I did not know at time, the principal's office. The thing that I look back on now and laugh so much about, is that he just left me and the teacher sitting there. We were just looking at each other. I didn't know what to say and he didn't know what to say. After what seemed like a minute, I asked the teacher was there anything else. When I told one of my friends this story, and she finished laughing, she said I should have told him, "I'm going to go on and go."

One Sunday, our Youth Pastor pulled me to one side and said, "Mrs. Soaries, I think you should know that your sons are tricking the teachers and switching classes at school. I just chuckled because, after all, they were just in the second grade. When I thought about it, he probably had a misunderstanding about what was happening at their school. The principal of the school was very creative, ingenious and fun. Since the school only went up to the second grade, she declared the second graders to be the "senior class," who were allowed to switch math class with the other second grade class. Just something different, but fun and creative. One evening at the dinner table, I said to one of my sons, "the Youth Pastor thinks you are switching classes at school and tricking your teachers." His reply to both of us was, "we are." My husband has surprisingly remained calm in this kind of situation. He said to my son, "tell me about it." My son said, "we dress alike because at recess we exchange our coats." (One of them wore red and the other wore blue.) He then said, "I like to go to gym twice on Fridays and my brother likes to go to the library twice on Wednesdays. Just in case our teachers thought they had figured out who we were, we would exchange coats so if they looked in the cloakroom they would know that the right color coat for the twin was there." Here I am thinking it's cute that they picked the same outfits to wear each day even though it was now their choice and I had stopped dressing them in the same outfits. Silly me! My husband and I made an appointment to meet with the creative, ingenious and fun principal. When we told her what we had discovered, she laughed so hard that she could hardly talk. She then said, "they are geniuses!" *O Lord!*

When my sons were in the third grade, I had traveled to Virginia for a speaking engagement which was very rare. When I returned, I listened to the voicemail messages on the home phone. There was a message from the principal of the school just checking on my son, Malcolm, to see if he was ok. I questioned my husband and asked what happened while I was gone. He explained that when he dropped Malcolm off at school that Friday morning, Malcolm didn't have his assignment because he needed a certain type of notebook. My son had waited until that morning to tell my husband about the certain composition book he needed for school, but my husband did not have time to pick one up at the last minute because he had a speech scheduled that morning.

This was the beginning of a new school year at a new school and Malcolm was feeling the pressure of the adjustment. It was always very important to him to have his assignments and have them done correctly. He had already missed a couple of assignments because he was not yet used to the new classroom procedures, and as a result, was being ridiculed by a few classmates for being unprepared. He decided that when my husband dropped him off and since there was an assembly program first thing when they walked in the school on Friday mornings, that he would pretend that he was going inside the school but would leave and go back home. He walked home. It had to be at least a mile. He had to cross a highway and walk through a wooded area. He said even a dog chased him. He knew that no one was home, but he just couldn't go inside that school and to that class unprepared again.

When his teacher realized that he was not in school, she went to his brother, Martin, to ask why he wasn't in school. Martin said he is in school because he did not see his brother leave. He just went to sit with his class for the assembly program. The teacher panicked and contacted the main office. You see, previously, my husband had informed the school of threats on his life from a person, and that the school had strict orders not to release his sons to anyone other than us without our permission. The FBI was involved and it was a very serious matter. They immediately contacted my husband who was on his way to the speaking engagement.

My husband said that when he pulled up to the school his heart sank because teachers and administrators were outside looking in the dumpsters and the woods behind the school calling Malcolm's name. The police had been called. My husband asked to see Martin and asked him where do you think Malcom is? He said, "he probably went home." My husband said that he just felt with the twin connection they had going on, he might know. His brother did not tell him what he was going to do. My husband drove home for what seemed like such an extremely long ride for him. When he got to the street where we lived and turned the corner, he could see our son sitting in front of the house. My husband said he was so thankful to see him he just got out of the car and sat down next to him. He didn't discuss anything at that moment only asked him was he ok. My husband took Malcolm with him to his speaking engagement. He says to this day he doesn't know what he said in the speech, he just knew that he was so very grateful that our son was alive and well. We later dealt with why attendance wasn't taken as soon as the children entered school on Fridays before the assembly programs. We also focused on the new school year, new school, new teacher, new classroom procedures, and new classmates to help our sons navigate a successful school year.

Always be prayerful about what it means for your children when they have to go to a different school for whatever reason. It can be traumatic for some children so be mindful of the adjustments they will have to make.

My husband was the 30th Secretary of State of New Jersey. He served with great distinction and we were very proud of him. One day, I received a call from my husband saying that our son, Martin, had called him a few times, but he was not able to take the call. I knew that he was away for a cabinet retreat with the Governor. He asked if I could please check with Martin, who was in school, to see what was going on. I called the school office to see if I could be connected to his classroom to speak to him. They graciously connected me and I asked what was happening. He informed me that he had made a deal with his fourth-grade teacher (who was an avid New Jersey Devils hockey fan) that if he got tickets to the championship game that night, they would not get homework. The entire class knew that the teacher was a fan and so Martin came up with the idea. Martin also knew that the governor was an avid fan and so he wanted my husband to ask the governor for tickets! During lunch break at the cabinet retreat, my husband told the governor what Martin had proposed to the teacher and the governor loved it so much that she offered four tickets for her game suite. The teacher, her husband, Martin and Malcolm went to the game that night. *O Lord!*

It is nice when your children are liked by others. The state troopers that were assigned to my husband as Secretary of State would take Malcolm and Martin laser tagging when they were off duty. When my sons were at the State House with my husband, they would ask the office assistant to make them coffee. They did not drink coffee but she didn't know that! *O Lord*, the perks of being the Secretary of State's sons!

Assignment

Enjoy these years. Enjoy this stage of your child being adorable, funny and excited about life. Take the time to do play dates and attend birthday parties. There will be many. We often say these are the best years of their lives. Make sure you contribute to those memories.

15

MIDDLE SCHOOL

When he was twelve years old, they went up to the festival, according to the custom. Luke 2:42 (NIV)

"A school usually including grades five to eight or six to eight."[6] This will be ages 11-14. This age group is often referred to as pre-teens. As a parent, you feel like you are still in control, but it won't be long. Seventh grade was an incredible school year for my sons. The school divided the middle school students into units. They were named for letters in the Greek alphabet. My sons were in the unit called Alpha. In my opinion, the teachers in this unit were some of the best teachers they ever had. There was the literature teacher. The curriculum she implemented mandated reading on a regular basis and explored a variety of topics. Their science teacher, who had a stern demeanor, was not as warmly received by most students, yet my sons absolutely loved her. The teacher that stood out the most to me was their English teacher. My sons, to this day, are prolific writers and have been since the seventh grade. When my sons were in middle school, I was taking some college courses, and while writing a paper, I asked the name of a show that they often watched. They asked me if I was looking for a "simile!" I don't know if they realized how much work was required of them being in the Alpha unit, but I think because they enjoyed the teachers so much there were no complaints. There were challenges with the math teacher, but three out of four is a good percentage. At the end of that school year, I invited the teachers to my home for lunch. Only two were able to come, but I took great pleasure in letting them know that I had prepared lunch out of total gratitude for the contribution they had made to my children's lives.

Middle school gave us one of the funniest stories we have about our sons. It was time for the spring concert and my sons were in the band. One played flute and the other played clarinet. I went to a music and art high school where I was the concert mistress. I took voice lessons in high school and later preformed as a lyric classical soprano. My husband's family was steeped in music and there was a great appreciation for the arts in both of our families. We were glad that our sons were studying and playing music. We came downstairs the day of the spring concert only to have our sons ask the question, "where are you all going?" We answered to the spring concert. They informed us that they had quit the band awhile back. *O Lord!* How come we were the last to know? Middle school age is getting you ready for high school.

Assignment

It may seem strange, but if you have a teacher(s) that you know has had a significantly positive impact in your child's life, don't just send a holiday gift or a gift at the end of the year, extend an invitation to your home and do lunch or dinner and talk to them face to face about the difference they made. Don't wait until the school year is over and let your child see firsthand what it looks like to let someone know how grateful you are for what they have done.

16
HIGH SCHOOL

Remember your Creator in the days of your youth, before the days of trouble come and the years approach when you will say, I find no pleasure in them. Ecclesiastes 12:1. (NIV)

I had my sons when I was 36. When my sons were teenagers, I was going through perimenopause. I felt so sorry for my husband. All of the hormones were raging in his family. I'm sure he had to call on the Lord often. Teenage years can be hard for parents, but you must remember that it is a changing and an adjustment time for the teenager. They are figuring things out. Their bodies aren't cooperating. Voice pitch changing, friends can act weird, all while they are trying to get work done in school and socialize.

The teenage years can be challenging. By the grace of God, my teenage years were not as challenging as they could have been. When I was a sophomore in high school, I was invited to a Friday night fellowship at Calvary Gospel Church in Newark, New Jersey. High School students were invited there to participate in a fun activity, meet other teenagers, and hear other teenagers share their testimonies which included the gospel. I gave my life to Christ at one of those Friday night meetings and it changed my life forever. It was called Conquerors Club based on Romans 8:37. I led my brother to Christ because I learned how to witness to others and share the gospel through that ministry. Some of the lifetime friendships I have are with those I met through Conquerors Club. So many ministers and ministries came out of that Conquerors Club. I know the Lord saved my life at that early age because only He knew where and what I would be if He had not saved my soul at that time.

Recently, a five-year old asked me when she thought she could date. She had already just told me she had a "crush" on someone! After I was able to close my mouth, I was able to tell her that I was allowed to go on my first date when I was 17 years old. Actually, my date took me to the movies, but we had to leave the theater before the movie was over because we had to catch a bus home so I wouldn't go past my curfew. When we arrived at my house, my mother was at the front door with the porch light on and asked me if I had a good time. *O Lord!* Of course, the five-year old is not going on a date, but the thought that she is thinking and asking about dating speaks to the fact that it is a new day!

Communication is the key in every stage of our child's life. It seems that it can be the most difficult time to communicate effectively when they are teenagers. They don't want to talk; they don't even want to answer. They think they know it all. So much happens during the teenage years that sometimes you may want to trade the children in, and the children may want to trade their parents in! Remember... they are your gifts! You have to hang in there.

They need you during these years even though they don't think that you know anything. If you find something that works and helps during these years, don't be shy about sharing it with other parents. They are going through just what you're going through. If you think your child may be depressed, if they won't talk to you, get them professional help. Again, this is the time when so much is changing for them. They are more prone to self-medicate with something! Keep your eyes open and keep prayed up. They likely need someone to talk to or to just listen to them. If the first counselor or therapist doesn't feel right for them, keep looking. Your child is worth it.

Teenagers have opinions. You might do well to have conversations with them about their opinions on certain subjects. Keep the dialogue going. You won't always agree, and they may even get frustrated if you ask too many questions or you don't understand, but keep the dialogue going. If you don't understand some of the "music" they listen to, try to have a discussion without judgment. Ask them questions to get them to think about what they listen to. Don't compromise your morals, just try to keep talking.

It will also come to pass that before they call, I will answer; and while they are still speaking, I will hear. Isaiah 65:24 (NKJV) HALLELUJAH!

Assignment

Pray, pray, pray. Pray so that they hear you praying. Pray with them when a test or a game or some special project is about to happen. Pray in their rooms, pray over their cars. Let their friends know that you will pray for them. Pray, pray, pray!!!

COLLEGE

But God chose the foolish things of the world to shame the wise; God chose the weak things of the world to shame the strong. 1 Corinthians 1:27 (NIV)

There is so much about the college experience with my children and even preparing for college that makes me always call on the scripture, *I Thessalonians 5:17,* "pray without ceasing." It's not just praying about the SAT or ACT; it is even the paperwork for FAFSA (Free Application for Federal Student Aid). The truth is, it is never too early to pray and prepare for all of these things. Our sons went to excellent public schools. We were very pleased. We enrolled them in SAT preparation classes. We created our own college tours. We went to five different states, and we took one of their best friends with us.

One son decided on a school in New York and the other a school in North Carolina. After one year, they both transferred to a university in Pennsylvania where they became roommates and graduated. My husband says they took the scenic route through college, but they graduated. Hallelujah!!!!! During the timeframe that I returned to college to pursue an advanced degree, I actually travelled to my sons' college once a week during one semester to encourage the one son, who needed at that time, to focus more. Those were some tough weeks for me. You are praying that they are focused and meeting their class requirements. You pray they don't drop classes and even more that you know about it if they do.

The college years weren't always challenging. My husband and I had quality time together. Most nights I slept well. One of my sons scored a thousand points on the basketball team in college. He was a great player and we really enjoyed going to the games. We got to see both sons when we went to games. My other son studied dance. Oh my goodness, he was amazing! He was in demand from senior dancers for their senior recitals. That is because he was amazing. I remember the audience literally gasping at one of his moves in a classical piece. It was just nice that they were together and close enough to drive and see them both perform.

I read a funny story one time where a mom was so impressed that whenever her son did return her call while he was in college, his reason for not answering the phone was because he was at the library. She was so impressed that he was at the library so much until she found out that the local club was called, "The Library." *O Lord!* This is their chance to have what they call "freedom." I say what they call freedom because even though they want freedom from things, they are not free from calling or texting for money on a regular basis. Stay connected, text scriptures, text "I love you," text, "how brilliant you are," and "you can do it."

I had a friend call recently and tell me that her son called her to tell her that he had been beaten up at a club. It doesn't matter ultimately what it was about; it was the fact that her son was away in school, she was not able to get to him and didn't know how serious it was. He was complaining of a headache and only to find out it was a mild concussion. We have to pray and trust God for their protection. *Psalm 46:7 (NIV), "The Lord Almighty is with us; the God of Jacob is our fortress."* As the mom and I talked, we couldn't stop saying that it could have been worse.

College is the next bridge to adulthood and responsibility. Pray, pray, pray. Pray without ceasing!

Rejoice always, pray continually, give thanks in all circumstances; for this is God's will for you in Christ Jesus. I Thessalonians 5:16-18 (NIV)

Assignment

Identify a college student that you will pray for the rest of this semester and send something to them. Find out from them or their parent what is their favorite snack. Be creative. Put a note in and just remind them of the plans God has for them. Young people away in college don't seem to answer the phone much, but if you can get their number and leave a message (hopefully, they will listen to it) it will mean a lot. Especially during exam time.

18

ADULT CHILDREN

Is anything too hard for the Lord? Genesis 18:14 (KJV)

My twin sons are adults now, have finished college and are working at what we call "good jobs." I love it because they work hard. Right after they graduated from college, I was more than happy for them to come home. I hear from many parents that their adult children are living at home. Some of them left home and needed to return home. Jobs in their field are not always available and they have to move in with roommates to make it financially. How do we balance parent vs. child in the household when the child is now an adult?

First of all, there will never come a time when they don't have to respect you. My sons have never disrespected me while speaking to me as adults. I'm not bragging. I'm grateful that they revere their dad and me in that way. Of course, they had their moments even as young children, but we got through those moments! What I'm trying to do now is balance respecting them as adults when it comes to some of the decisions they make. I have to step back when they are not moving at the pace that I think is appropriate.

What happens when your adult child texts you and says that he or she did not get the promotion they interviewed for? They were sure they were going to get it. The days are over for wanting to fix everything. They are adults now. You listen, you let them know that they will get through it and when they calm down, they will maybe even look at what they could have done or said better in the interview. The one thing that can't happen is they can't take it out on you. They can't display anger because you are not saying the things they want to hear. This is when it becomes very clear whether or not you are a helicopter parent, "a parent who is overly involved in the life of his or her child."[7] That means you are watching and operating every move. Your adult child doesn't have to make decisions because you will make the decision. Your adult child doesn't have to fix it because you will fix it. Your adult child doesn't even have to lose sleep over things because you will take care of the sleepless nights. Of course, this helicopter hovering started long before adulthood, but you will see more evidence of it in their adult years. Remember, adult children are getting closer to the years where they may have to take care of you in one way or another.

A friend shared a story that really helped me. Her daughter was gradually moving to New York City from New Jersey. One Monday morning, the daughter decided to take a bunch of her items to her new apartment in NYC in several large bags by train. Her mother told her that was too much to handle on a train and offered to take the bags to NYC by car the following weekend. Her daughter was adamant about taking all the bags to NYC that day by train and my friend reluctantly drove her to the train station that morning. At the train station, my friend watched as her daughter struggled toward the platform with all the bags. Her daughter just kept saying "I'll be fine, Mommy. My friend said that she was so afraid for her daughter's safety with all those bags. Before she drove away from the station, she prayed, "Dear God, please take care of my child. Please send an angel to help her…" During her one-hour commute to work, my friend got a text message from her daughter. It said, "Mommy, I met an angel on the train!! A lady helped me with my bags, got a seat for me, and we talked all the way to NYC!!" My friend said she got chills while reading the message, "an angel" her daughter said!! *O Lord!* When my friend talked to her daughter, she learned that the lady chatted with her about health, wellness, and the goodness of God and gave her a business card. My friend called the "angel" after work and thanked her for helping her daughter on the train. My friend developed a friendship with the "angel." They met for lunch, talked about spiritual growth and their adult children.

Here was a time where it was difficult for a parent to let go and fall back when their adult child made a decision the parent did not agree with. Let your adult child be an adult! This is a great example of letting go and letting God! …and the power of prayer!!

Prayer: God you know that I tried to be the best parent you would have me to be. I am the first to admit that I wasn't perfect, but you did not expect me to be. Now that they are adults help me to really give them over to you.

Assignment

This is a key time to keep the dialogue going. Do lunch, do dinner, you pay sometimes, they pay sometimes. After all they are adults. Continue to listen to their dreams and aspirations. Be attentive to what they talk about and make sure you pray with them and for them.

19
SIBLINGS

When the news reached Pharaoh's palace that Joseph's brothers had come, Pharaoh and all his officials were pleased. Genesis 45:16 (NIV)

In Genesis, chapters 37-50 is the familiar story of Joseph, which is a very rich story with many lessons. It is the story of Joseph and his coat of many colors. Jacob had twelve sons and Joseph was the next to last of his sons. The Bible says that Joseph was Jacob's favorite and he gave him a beautiful coat. As parents, we often contribute to the core of jealousy established between siblings. I realized that my mother and father worked on a balance between my twin brother and me. I, in turn, made sure that I was sensitive to my twin sons. You may not think that they notice, but they do.

When we read the story of Joseph and his brothers, we see the pinnacle of jealousy among siblings. We ultimately want our children to love each other. Jealousy is a human feeling within, but it doesn't just go away because you say to your child don't be jealous of your brother or your sister. A child should be encouraged to turn feelings of envy to feelings of being proud. It doesn't happen right away, so you have to work on it. I worked very hard on making sure that I gave equal time and attention to both of my sons. They may not have recognized it, but I did. I still work on it, now. Where did I get that from?... my mother who was also the mother of twins.

I have often heard an only child say that they wish they had a sibling. I have also often heard those with siblings say that they wish they were the only child! I absolutely loved having siblings. My two older sisters are 9 and 10 years older than me and my twin brother. I have always been very close to my brother. When people ask, "are we close," I say yes! However, by other people's standards, they may not consider how we could really be close. We live in different states, we don't talk every day on the phone, I don't auto-matically know when something is bothering him, but I believe we are close. I love and respect him so much. He is one of the kindest, devoted Christian, caring persons I know. I realize that my parents set the standard for being connected and loving as siblings. This is the parent's responsibility.

From a young age, I always emphasized to my sons to love and take care of each other. They were told not to let others bring conflict to their relationship. I did not realize to what degree they took it until we were on vacation one year and my husband got frustrated with one of my sons. My other son stood up to his dad to challenge him, and when asked why he did that, he stated you told me to always take care of my brother. *O Lord!*

I don't understand any parent comparing one child to the other, pitting siblings against each other at any age, allowing jeal-ousy, encouraging arguments or not speaking to each other. I don't understand it at all. We were taught to love our siblings. As adult siblings, there may be things we don't agree on. An example is that one of my sisters is of a different faith than the rest of us. I love my sister so much. She is my oldest sister. She's funny, talented, creative, supportive and I can't wait to run new and creative ideas and recipes by her. Remember, as a parent after you are gone, you want to know that your children love each other so much that they will be there for each other through the rest of their lives. So often when the matriarch and the patriarch of the family passes away, the children don't cultivate that same connection and so communication and connections can end between siblings.

While earning my undergraduate degree in counseling, we studied Alfred Adler who was a medical doctor, psychotherapist, and founder of the school of individual psychology. Adler believed birth order has unique advantages and disadvantages and that each birth order position has a unique set of personality traits.[8] The information provided below gives you a general idea of the characteristics of birth order and how it effects siblings.

BIRTH ORDER	CHARACTERISTICS
Firstborn	A firstborn child may tend to be an overachiever and a perfectionist who wants to please their parents.
Middle Child	A middle child may feel left out due to lack of attention from family. They may tend to be people-pleasers and develop a stronger relationship with friends.
Youngest Child	The youngest child tends to be free-spirited because parents have relaxed the rules. May be spoiled and identified as the "baby of the family."
Only Child	The only child tends to be mature for their age and can be seen as a leader. They have no competition and generally have the full attention of their parents.
Twins	Due to the actual time of birth, when twins are identified as youngest and oldest, they may take on the characteristics of the youngest and oldest child.

Assignment

April 20 is National Sibling Day in the United States and Canada. My brother was first to inform my sisters and me of the fact. He posted pictures and a special tribute to us on Facebook one year. This year, he called us and shares some funny memories of growing up. Celebrate your siblings with something creative on that date. If you do not have siblings, identify the one you love like siblings and celebrate them.

20
FRIENDS

A friend loves at all times... Proverbs 17:17(NIV)

The Bible clearly states that in order to have friends you must show yourself friendly. Proverbs 18:24. My husband often says that if you have one good friend you are blessed. I thank God that I have a few, but over the years I have learned that just to have a few is a blessing, as well. My personal best girlfriends are women who love God, love their husbands, if they are married, and love their children. What that means for me is that we have something in common. I can always share things about my children when I get upset or frustrated and my friends will listen. Sometimes they will fuss with me and even get angry if I don't take their advice. But when I am over it, my friends are over it. They don't stop speaking to my children and don't hold anything against them. One of my dearest friends asked me to speak to one of her daughters in hopes that I could help her with some frustrations she was having. This happened before I earned my degree in counseling, so my response to her was how can I speak to your daughter when I am having challenges with my own children? It did, however, make me feel good that she had confidence in me that I could help her situation. That's a friend.

As parents, we are always focused on our children's friends. Who are they attracted to? What personalities are they drawn to?

Peer pressure definitely comes into play. How badly do they want to fit in with the "popular kids?" Are they drawn to friends that seem prone to get in trouble or make bad decisions? In my day, whoever my friends were, my parents knew their names, where they lived, and probably what their parents did for a living. Maybe what they do for a living is now "too much information," but you need to have phone numbers to connect with the parents of the friends that your children hang out with. Back in the day, our parents had to actually MEET our friends' parents!

This upbringing, I believe, is probably why I don't usually go to many of my friends' homes as an adult. It doesn't mean there is something wrong with their homes, it has just become a way of life for me. In return, I do not have a lot of people in my home.

I have a friend who shared one day that her children were not allowed to attend sleepovers and neither was I. She even shared that after leaving her daughter at a swim party SOMETHING told her to go back only to see her child fall in an above-ground pool and she couldn't swim. My friend rocked that above ground pool until water and her daughter came out. The owner was yelling, "you're going to break my pool!!" My friend responded, "YES!" Listen to the voice, that intuition, that gut feeling. Our children want to be liked by their friends and they don't want you embarrassing them around their friends, but you probably know who is a good friend for them to have. Remember you couldn't always identify who were the best friends for you to be around.

My personal story is about my oldest sister, Velda, who was away at college. When it was time to return home for Thanksgiving break, she wanted to ride with friends, and my mother said, "No." My sister was hurt and embarrassed. It meant everything to her to be able to ride home with her friends. My sister also had the pressure of her friends wanting her to ride with them. I was so impressed when I heard the story that my sister was obedient and took the bus home. The very next morning my sister answered the phone and heard our aunt scream, "...is this Velda??!!" My sister responded, "Yes," but since my aunt was so emotional, Velda handed the phone to our mother. She then found out that the friends she wanted to ride home with had all been killed in a car accident on their way home!! *O Lord!* What if it had been more important to impress her friends than to be obedient to her parents' instructions? We don't always know if what we are feeling is right about situations and friends, but we do know that the Spirit will guide us, so it is crucial to stay prayed up and connected to the leading of the Spirit.

I have tried over the years to ensure my sons are "good" friends. I encouraged them to be the leader in the group. Now, it doesn't always feel good being the one that says, "this thing that we are about to do is just dumb!" But in years to come you may be thankful for life-altering decisions that were made because someone had the courage to say, "don't do it." You want your child to be the reliable friend. The Bible says in Proverbs 18:24 (NIV), *"One who has unreliable friends soon comes to ruin, but there is a friend who sticks closer than a brother."* If our children have a relationship with the Lord, they do have a friend who will be with them always. That friend always listens and gives direction. In other words, pray about it. That friend doesn't judge and loves all the way. Jesus is a good friend to have.

Assignment

Identify your best friends. Find a book about friends to give them or send a card that expresses your gratefulness to have a "real friend."

21

BULLYING

He giveth power to the faint; and to them that have no might he increaseth strength. Isaiah 40:29(KJV)

"I've learned that people will forget what you said, people will forget what you did, but people will never forget how you made them feel."[9] (Maya Angelou)

Be mindful of any change in your child's personality, such as being frustrated a lot, moody, staying to themselves, not eating, disrespecting you, etc. It could be a number of things, but make sure you are sensitive to them and talk about the possibility of being bullied. Many times, they don't want you to do anything about it because they feel it will only make matters worse if you speak or do something about it. What a horrible feeling to not want to go to school every day, for fear you will run into the bully that seeks you out!

There are different levels of bullying. There can be crazy reasons for bullying. Your child can be bullied because they dress well or speak well. They can be bullied because of a special talent. They can be bullied because of who their parents are. Unfortunately, not only can a child be bullied by their peers, they can also be bullied by adults. What kind of world do we live in when it feels good to do things that hurts someone else!?

Here's another thing to consider…make sure your child is not the bully! *O Lord!* You can definitely do something about that. When your child is the bully, you must address their insecurities, which cause them to bully others. Talk to them about what it means to stand up for themselves and for others that are being bullied. Have a ritual of affirmations that you have your child repeat about themselves. I am loved, I am beautiful, I am smart, I am creative, I am a child of the King!

National Statistics on Bullying[10] (2017)

* **Been Bullied**
  * 28% of U.S. students in grades 6–12 experienced bullying
  * 20% of U.S. students in grades 9–12 experienced bullying.

* **Bullied Others**
  * Approximately 30% of young people admit to bullying others in surveys.

* **Seen Bullying**
  * 70.6% of young people say they have seen bullying in their schools.
  * 70.4% of school staff have seen bullying. 62% witnessed bullying two or more times in the last month and 41% witness bullying once a week or more.
  * When bystanders intervene, bullying stops within 10 seconds 57% of the time.

- **Been Cyberbullies**
  - 9% of students in grades 6–12 experienced cyberbullying
  - 15% of high school students (grades 9–12) were electronically bullied in the past year.
  - However, 55.2% of LGBTQ students experienced cyberbullying.

Assignment

Make a sign or order a sign with this scripture. Put it in your child's room so that they can meditate on it for years to come: *If God be for us, who can be against us? Romans 8:32 (KJV)*

22

MENTAL HEALTH

"Thou wilt keep him in perfect peace, whose mind is stayed on thee: because he trusteth in thee." Isaiah 26:3 (KJV)

When I was growing up, we didn't address the issues around mental health head on. If a child couldn't keep still in class, we just referred to it as "he or she has ants in their pants." If a child seemed sad, we just left them alone or tried to convince them that they had too much to be happy about. Now we know of Attention Deficit Disorder (ADD), Attention-Deficit Hyperactivity Disorder (ADHD) and other approaches to mental health, and even medications. I would encourage you, as a parent, to research as much as you can when your child has been diagnosed or labeled with a diagnosis. We now know that diet contributes to so many things. The sugar, sugar, sugar in their diet can take anyone into a different personality. Not saying that it is always the case, but fast foods and the hormones used to make chicken and cows grow faster can affect the person eating the chicken. You know that there is a noticeable difference in a child's activity after they have consumed a soda, some candy or cookies.

If you start out having your child eat carrots for snacks, have them drink water when they are thirsty, after a while, they will ask for carrots when they want a snack or water when they are thirsty. It may be hard to believe, but it's true. Of course, when they try that cookie or candy, they enter a new atmosphere, but monitor it. Balance it. Help them to get a good night's sleep by not allowing so much sugar and additives. They are in a better mood in the morning and your day is better. During the teenage years, they want to stay up later than ever and that affects getting up for school. Moms, all of the above apply to you. When you feel as if something is just not right, do something about it. If you notice that being in church helps you feel so good, but the rest of the week you are down, you should seek professional help. You are worth taking care of yourself. You will be a better mom and parent because of it.

We don't want our children classified as needing special education services. We see it as a stigma. We don't want to hear any of the labels. Sometimes we don't even want to hear about migraine headaches, but we have to address the things that affect our children head on. Don't put blinders on. Pray, get with your prayer partners and pray, but if you see they are struggling, make it a point to find out what it is. My heart was so heavy when I heard of an eight-year old who tried to commit suicide twice. What took him to this place? Thank God he had someone in his village who was ready to pray him through and medically address the issue. Don't ignore it. It doesn't just go away.

Nay in all these things we are more than conquerors through Him that loved us! Romans 8:37(KJV)

Assignment

Do some research on mental health. Become more informed on what is happening to our children and parents. You won't become an authority, but prayerfully, you will become more sensitive to things that may be happening in your own home.

23
CHURCH

Not forsaking the assembling of ourselves together, as the manner of some is; but exhorting one another. Hebrews 10:25 (KJV)

Church is such an important part of the life of a Christian. For years, in the African American tradition, church was all we had to deal with life's issues. Children learned how to deliver speeches in their Sunday school plays. You were taught how to address an older person with a firm handshake. We learned what was appropriate dress for church, or should I say, what was not appropriate. Church was where you learned to respect your elders and the Pastor. It was the ultimate place to learn to sit still and be quiet for a minimum of two hours. You could try to listen and understand the sermon after all of the music was over. You could get a pencil and write on the program, you could lay on your parents' shoulder and take a nap, but you were going to be in church and be quiet.

As my husband often says, we went to church when we were young because we wanted to live. You knew that no matter how late you came in Saturday night you had to be in church on Sunday. We made friends in church. We enjoyed participating in the youth activities. I enjoyed singing in the choir. We still had no say so on whether or not we were going. Our parents took us to church. That was an example of commitment all by itself. It is so different nowadays. Our children are not committed or excited about going to church. So many distractions in their lives. So many things competing for their attention.

We have a responsibility to be very careful about how we talk about the church and by that, I mean the people in the church. When our children hear us talking about the Pastor and the people in the church it stays with them. *O Lord!* Remember, it also stays with them when they hear us talking about the goodness of the Lord, the great sermon the preacher preached, how wonderful the music was, and that we are praying for our brothers and sisters in church. Gossip has no place in or out of the church. We want our children to have such a relationship with God as a result of being in church that even if they stop going when they become older, there is something that will compel them to want to go back. Even more important than that is to maintain a relationship with God.

Only the Lord knows where and how the church is moving with worship for our young people. We are seeing different ways even now that the "church" is present. Here's the bottom line. We want them to know Jesus as their personal Savior and Lord. Live your life to be the witness they need to want to be in church and most importantly have a personal relationship with Christ!

It is so important for the church to make sure the children and young people feel connected. Don't wait until they become young adults to put them in ministries and auxiliaries. You would be amazed to see what they can contribute during their early years.

Mentoring is necessary, and yes, even in the church. Identify a child who might be interested in your profession and let them "shadow" you and hang out with you on the job, if only for a day.

Assignment

Write a note or send an email message to your Pastor or someone in leadership in your church thanking them for what they do to make the church what it is. Then send a note to a musician, a nurse, an usher or even those who may work in the kitchen. They all make it work and they are grateful for words of appreciation.

24

SOCIAL MEDIA

Not that I speak in respect of want; for I have learned in whatsoever state I am, therewith to be content. Philippians 4:11 (KJV)

Only the Lord knows where we are going from here. When I was growing up, if you were driving to a destination to visit someone, you got the directions from them and you wrote it down. If you got lost, you had to stop and ask someone. God forbid you had someone following you because if you got separated, oh well.

I remember one day not long after getting a cell phone and not yet learning about text messaging, I didn't notice the messages on it. I did not pay that option much attention because I thought it was just something weird happening with my phone. Only to find out by asking my sons that those were incoming text messages! Now we text each other and we don't even have to use our fingers to send them. Just speak into the phone and the words that we want to say will be sent. We send the letters, LOL, for "laughing out loud" or we send a yellow smiley face, as if we needed less conversation with our children. *O Lord!*

There are so many social media platforms now. Facebook, Twitter, Instagram, Snapchat, etc. There seems to be something new coming out every time I feel like I have learned the last one. Parents, learn how to use social media and talk to your child about it. Ask them how it works. Ask them what they think is the advantage of using it. Try to get your children to think about what they do. Let them know that things they put on social media today can show up years later even if you deleted it. Think about the fact that some of the silly things you did in your past, you wouldn't want to show up in a job interview today!

I struggle with text messaging because it seems to have taken the place of us talking and having a decent conversation with not just our children, but with family members and friends, in general. When my sons were in college, they would never answer when I called, but if I texted, I would probably get a response.

I am from South Carolina. We like to talk. We like to talk a lot. We have to go all the way around the barn to say what we have to say. I can't say everything I need to say in a text message. I also think that sometimes more than a one-word answer is merited. Another problem with texting is that people can't always know the tone of a text message. Thoughts are misunderstood at times and interpreted differently than intended.

Conversations use to be around the dinner table. Children heard life lessons, history and current events. Talking and sharing gives a sense of the good and the bad. Talking to our children and listening helps us to know what and who to pray for. There are chat groups on our phones that we text our opinions to, but when possible, consider using conference calls with family. Let's talk!

Assignment

Text a scripture to your child several times a week for a month to encourage them to commit the verse to memory. Ask them about the verse from time to time.

25
HOLIDAY TRADITIONS

Each year you and your family are to eat them in the presence of the
Lord your God at the place he will choose. Deuteronomy 15:20 (NIV)

We traditionally believe that no matter what the holiday is, it
is better when celebrated with family and friends. My memories of
holidays as a young child were very special. Family, food, laughter
and music. My mother was an amazing cook. My dad worked
part-time at the Elks club as a waiter when I was very young in
South Carolina. He had a bachelor's degree and was a principal at
an elementary school, but this was his way of getting extra food
for his family after a catering event. I learned from my dad how
to set a table, serve a table and even carve meat with and against
the grain. We got quality food after those events and we looked
forward to it. When we entertained in our home the table was set
correctly with linens, silverware and crystals, which may not have
been expensive, but the table was set correctly. I must admit that
it is a point of contention for me when I see a table set incorrectly.
Lord help me.

At any family gathering we ate great food. There was so much
laughter at the table and after dessert we would gather around
the piano. My mother would play hymns or Christmas carols at
Christmas, but we would always sing "He Knows How Much You
Can Bear." Mommy, who was an accomplished pianist, would

always play Duke Ellington's, "Sophisticated Lady and String of Pearls" by Glenn Miller. Afterwards, she would play ballroom music so that my dad could dance with my sisters and me. My dad was such a smooth dancer. He led us on the floor as if we were in a dance contest. This happened at every family gathering.

The best part of the evening and the last thing we would do is sing the song "Tell Me Why" written by Marty Gold words by Al Alberts. The lyrics are:

Tell me why the stars do shine
Tell me why the ivy twines
Tell me why the sky's so blue
And then I'll tell you just why I love you
Because God made the stars to shine
Because God made the ivy twine
Because God made the sky's so blue
Because God made you, that's why I love you...[11]

We sang this song in four-part harmony. Mommy would accompany us on the first verse and then we would sing the second verse acappella. It brings tears to my eyes every time I think about it. While writing this book, I went on YouTube to listen to some variations of the song and sent them to my siblings. All three of them contacted me and told me how special it was to them to be reminded of the song. It was special to me to know how it was special to them, also!

A few years ago, we had a family gathering at my home and the three different generations that were there were asked to come up with their own interpretation of "Tell Me Why." You can imagine we had everything from acappella harmony to hip hop! It was wonderful! If you start singing the song around many of my family members today, they recognize the song even if they don't know it all. *O Lord!*

Assignment

Establish a tradition with the family. It doesn't have to be on a holiday, but holidays can make it easier when families tend to get together. As my sons got older, we have tried to go to the movies after dinner on Thanksgiving. It could be everyone contributing a paragraph about what they are thankful for that year and it could culminate into a book that you self-publish. Do something, start something! It will bring smiles in years to come.

26
THE PAINTING

For I know the plans I have for you," declares the Lord, "plans to prosper you and not to harm you, plans to give you hope and a future."
Jeremiah 29:11 (NIV)

I have to believe that this inspiration to share my thoughts was given to me from God. I believe it will bless other mothers when I share it and that even ensures more that God gave it to me. If I were to paint a painting that portrayed exactly what I see my sons' lives in the present and future, it would look something like this:

I would stand in front of an easel and paint this painting on a canvas. The painting would show one of my sons probably as the CEO of Vogue Italia. His gift in fashion along with his brilliance in business and even foreign language would qualify him for this position. He would be well respected in the fashion world for his creative gifts and for his integrity. In my painting he is active in a church, has a strong relationship with the Lord and he is consistently telling others about having a personal relationship with God. In my painting, he is happy and healthy. He manages his money well and is able to give to others accordingly. He has great friends. He is very happy with his life!

In my painting of my other son, he is the head coach of the basketball team at a Division I College. It would probably be Duke

University since that is one of his favorite college teams. He would love coaching since he is so good at it. He would be changing the lives of the young men on the team just by mentoring them. He would give a lot of himself to the community and even do mission work. He would consistently go to church and have a personal relationship with the Lord. In my painting, he would be happy and healthy. He would manage his money well and be able to give to others accordingly. He has great friends. He is very happy with his life!

That is my painting. The painting that shows what I see as success for them. I am happy! I then realized that I had missed so much in my painting. If I looked harder, I had missed that they are alive. They are both very respectful of my husband, me and others. They are absolutely brilliant. They both have jobs and they work very hard at what they do. I missed on the painting where it showed that they are so funny and enjoy laughing and being with their parents. I missed that they love children and are very compassionate towards others. They love their extended family. I missed that they are really good friends to others. I missed that they have their own relationship with God. They are happy!

Unfortunately, we get so caught up in what the perfect "painting" of what life should look like for our children, that we miss who they already are and the greatness that is in them already. *O Lord!*

Jesus told his disciples *"…whoever believes in me will do the works I have been doing, and they will do even greater things than these, because I am going to the Father." John 14:12 (NIV)*

Assignment

Imagine or even draw your own painting. No matter what your child's age, put in the picture who you desire them to be. Then in the painting identify who they actually are and be grateful.

27

PRAY WITHOUT CEASING

¹⁶Rejoice always, ¹⁷pray continually, ¹⁸give thanks in all circumstances; for this is God's will for you in Christ Jesus. 1 Thessalonians 5:16-18 (NIV)

As a young Christian when I first became familiar with this verse, I imagined that Paul was saying to pray 24/7. As a new Christian, you are zealous and want to do everything to please the Lord. I thought to myself, I will never be able to do it. I looked up "without ceasing" in a commentary. "The Greek word for "without ceasing" in 1 Thessalonian 5:17 is adialeiptos, which doesn't mean nonstop — but actually means constantly recurring. In other words, we can punctuate our moments with intervals of recurring prayer..." "We pray without ceasing. Every secret wish is a prayer."¹²

Let me tell you something, to be a parent means you need to pray as much as you can and then pray some more. Pray aloud, pray through the house, pray with your children. Have them pray. I prayed in the car with my sons on the way to school. We took turns praying. My husband often recognizes a woman at our church that reinforced praying when teaching them in Vacation Bible School. They learned how to pray at home. When they would stay in the home of one of my best friends and her husband, Aunt Faye and Uncle Stewart, they heard them pray and then they were required to pray. That was their Aunt and Uncle's standard. Every now and then my sons will ask me to pray about something. Sometimes, they say to me, "Ma, I know God did that." That's their prayers being answered. *O Lord!*

You will pray through tears and praise. I even had a friend suggest that we get knee pads so that we can be on our knees as much as possible. As a result, I had foam knee pads designed and imprinted with *"Mothers Determined To Pray."* I encouraged parents to make sure their children see them praying on the knee pads.

There will be days, months and years when you will wonder does God hear your prayers. Let me assure you, He does! Don't stop praying and don't get so stuck on what you think the answer should exactly be that you miss how the Lord is answering your prayer.

Call unto me, and I will answer thee, and show thee great and mighty things, which thou knowest not. Jeremiah 33:3 (KJV)

Assignment

Start a journal with prayer requests. Make sure you put answered prayers in it. I recommend "The Partner Prayer Journal" by Becky Tirabassi. There are many others available.

MOTHERS DETERMINED TO PRAY

"Evening and morning and at noon, I will pray and cry aloud and He shall hear my voice." Psalm 55:17 (KJV)

This book was written as I reflected on my years as a mother. I love being a mother. I love my sons with all my heart. I have used the guideline to love as a mother using I Corinthians 13 as a standard. When I reflect on things that I did as a mother, there are some things that I wish I had done differently, and I am not perfect, but there are so many things, by the grace of God, I know I did well.

I am sharing how I approached some things as a mom over the years. I am not saying, of course, this is the way you need to do it. I received so much advice from the beginning up and until now on what I should do in certain situations as a mom. Let me tell you, firsthand, that I am careful and prayerful with the advice I give. I have had people tell me what they wouldn't put up with if they were me. I promise you; you don't know what you would put up with unless you are in the exact situation. I have had advice from people that don't even have children. Their perspective may be valid, and I am not saying that their advice is not good advice, but what was best for me the 30 years that I have been a mom was from people in my life that loved my children and prayed for them. I mean, prayer warrior prayers. I mean "sho' nuff" prayer warriors.

I hope this book encourages you to not only pray for your children but to pray for other children. Pray for children in your family, in your church, your co-workers' children, children in the neighborhood, children in other countries. Every mother does not have some of the experiences I share in this book, but they need our prayers.

My husband and I tried for almost two years after we got married to get pregnant. He was traveling a lot. I was a few pounds overweight, I was up in years, all things that doctors and people would say are a factor of why it may be hard to get pregnant. I knew it was true, but I also knew for a fact that it happens when God says so. I took so many early pregnancy tests that I should have bought stock in the companies! *O Lord!* Every month I was saying "doesn't that line look blue?" I had to wait on the Lord. *But, they that wait upon the Lord!!!!!!*

It was out of nowhere that I said to myself this is past the time of the month and let me get to a clinic and get tested. When the doctor came out and said my test was positive, I started crying. She thought I was upset. My husband was out of town and when he called again, I was crying and told him I was pregnant. By this time he wanted me to go to my doctor and get blood work done to be sure, but I knew. So happy!

My husband announced one Sunday in church that we were pregnant. He said that he was praying for twins. Of course, some-one heard it wrong, and thought he said we were having twins, and the person took it upon herself to call my doctor to inform her that we were having twins. (See, that's when the praying needed to start, people can get things so wrong) My doctor called me quite upset because she wanted to know how I found out it was twins. I told her I did not find out, but he was praying for twins because we were up in age and he said let's have two and be done.

I actually told her I felt I was going to disappoint my husband because he was telling everyone he was praying for twins. I am fraternal twin, and having twins was not supposed to be a possibility. She told me it wasn't too soon to do a sonogram, she would see the baby on the screen, hear the heartbeat and all would be well. I could not wait for the day to come. I went in first and the technician said he would come back and get my husband. When the technician prepared me and turned on the machine, I saw him turn his head sideways. He said, "Mrs. Soaries, are you on fertility pills?" I said no, but with a not so pleasant reflection in my voice I said, "why are you asking me that?" He said, "I see two!" I said, "please go get my husband." When my husband walked in the room, I had my hands over my face and said, "Soaries, it's two!" He said "I tried to tell you!!" Can you imagine me calling my family and friends prefacing my statement that this is not a joke! I am having twins! *O Lord!*

All you can do is try to be the best parent you can be. Your parents did good and also made mistakes. My husband and I had expressed some of the things that we did wrong when we were growing up. Of course, we did not tell them everything, but shame on you if you want them to think you were perfect all the way. It won't kill you to tell your children you are sorry when you have made a mistake or should have handled something differently. I'm glad my children know I have their backs and if someone wants to say something negative about them, I won't participate in the conversation. That does something for your child to know that you have their back.

I hope reading this book helps you to reflect, smile and even bring good memories of when you were growing up. This book was written to encourage you to smile, consider the Word of God and pray, pray, pray! Fervent prayer is what got me through being a Mother. *O Lord!*

Mothers Determined To Pray
Saturday Mornings, 8:00am - 8:15am EST
712-432-0075 Access Code 311966#
Go to <u>*www.motherspray.com*</u> *for prayer requests, praise reports, and testimonials…or to just stay in touch.*

APPENDIX

[1] "Gift." *Merriam-Webster.com Dictionary*, Merriam-Webster, https://www.merriam-webster.com/dictionary/gift. Accessed 25 Apr. 2020.

[2] Helget, N. L. (2015). *Stillwater*. Boston: Mariner Books, Houghton Mifflin Harcourt.

[3] Wikipedia contributors. "This Little Light of Mine." Wikipedia, The Free Encyclopedia. Wikipedia, The Free Encyclopedia, 7 Apr. 2020. Web. 1 May. 2020

[4] Wikipedia contributors. "It takes a village." *Wikipedia, The Free Encyclopedia*. Wikipedia, The Free Encyclopedia, 27 Jan. 2020. Web.

[5] Murkoff, H. E., Mazel, S., & Neppe, C. (2018). *What to expect when you're expecting*. Sydney, N.S.W.: HarperCollins Publishers.

[6] "Middle school." *Merriam-Webster.com Dictionary*, Merriam-Webster, "Middle school." *Merriam-Webster.com Dictionary*, Merriam-Webster, https://www.merriam-webster.com/dictionary/middle%20school. Accessed 25 Apr. 2020.

[7] "Helicopter parent." *Merriam-Webster.com Dictionary*, Merriam-Webster, https://www.merriam-webster.com/dictionary/helicopter%20parent. Accessed 25 Apr. 2020.

[8] Adler, Alfred. *The Collected Clinical Works of Alfred Adler.* Classical Adlerian Translation Project, 2002. http://www.adlerian.us/homepage.htm. Accessed 31 Mar. 2020.

[9] Harper. "21 Of Maya Angelou's Best Quotes To Inspire." *Harper's BAZAAR*, Harper's BAZAAR, 6 June 2018, www.harpersbazaar.com/culture/features/a9874244/best-maya-angelou-quotes/. Accessed 27 Apr. 2020.

[10] National Center for Education Statistics and Bureau of Justice Statistics, *School Crime Supplement – PDF*, 2011. https://www.stopbullying.gov/resources/facts#stats. Accessed 31 Mar. 2020.

[11] Wikipedia contributors. "Tell Me Why (1951 song)." *Wikipedia, The Free Encyclopedia*. Wikipedia, The Free Encyclopedia, 18 Sep. 2019. Web.

[12] Barry C. Black, *"Can one truly 'pray without ceasing?"* https://www.washingtontimes.com/news/2015/nov/29/power-of-prayer-can-one-truly-pray-without-ceasing/. Accessed 31 Mar. 2020.

Martin and Malcolm

Made in the USA
Coppell, TX
30 October 2020